The Light of Consciousness

The Light of Consciousness

Explorations in Transpersonal Psychology

Richard D. Mann

STATE UNIVERSITY OF NEW YORK PRESS
ALBANY

Published by
State University of New York Press, Albany

Printed in the United States of America

For information, address State University of New York Press
State University Plaza, Albany, N.Y. 12246

Library of Congress Cataloging in Publication Data
Mann, Richard D. (Richard Dewey), 1933–
The light of consciousness
Bibliography: p.
1. Psychology, Religious. 2. Myth. 3. Muktananda, Swami, 1908–1982. Citśakti Vilās. 4. Spiritual life (Hinduism). I. Title. II. Title: Transpersonal psychology. III. Series.
BL53.M3678 1984 150.19 83-18088
ISBN 0-87395-905-1
ISBN 0-87395-906-X (pbk.)

CONTENTS

PREFACE

We create, and we are created by, our myths. It is through our personal and collective myths that we explore our own identity, the nature of the world around us, and our connection with past and future. Transpersonal psychology is a myth in the making—a myth that captures the central meaning of the many lives being transformed through self-discovery. The bond I now feel with those who write in transpersonal psychology is formed by a sense of our moving along convergent routes toward a common goal.

It wasn't long ago, however, that I felt compelled to take issue with someone who was talking about her life, first as a psychologist in France and later as a devotee of an Indian spiritual teacher. I interrupted in order to put on record one of the central assertions of my own world view: "Well, I don't believe in God or anything like that." I expected some sort of controversy to ensue, but she just laughed and said, "Oh, I understand, but what I mean by God is just whatever one spends the greatest amount of time thinking about. So, really, everyone has some god or other, don't you think?"

I had to agree, and later, when I pondered what my own god might be, I saw how intensely I had concentrated upon and indeed deified certain "factors" in group process. I had worked for twenty years at Harvard and Michigan, studying and interpreting the latent causes of what was happening in T-groups, classrooms, and self-analytic groups. The "cause" for which I was always probing, beneath the surface layer of denials and avoidance, was anger. Only when anger or resentment had been identified as a major cause of what was happening could I conclude that the group and I had arrived at the object of our inquiry. Anger, it appeared, was certainly pervasive and powerful enough to be the god of my interpersonal reality.

As I pondered this, the mists cleared, revealing an Olympian hierarchy of gods. How puny my god—anger—seemed to be, how dwarfed by other gods far more fundamental and worthy of the constant focus of my attention. Love, freedom, truth, and peace were among the higher gods overshadowing this minor god of anger to which I had devoted so much of my adult life. The myth that had served me so well seemed suddenly unnecessary and ready to be discarded. But how?

The process of reshaping my personal myth was greatly affected by a series of encounters with a great Indian saint, Swami Muktananda of Ganeshpuri. This book is an effort to portray the interaction of two world views, his and mine. To present his, I have chosen a series of events that document his spiritual evolution and transformation. These events are drawn from his autobiography, *Play of Consciousness*. In the primary sequence of this text he describes his direct and shifting meditative experiences of what he calls "the Blue Pearl."[1]

In presenting the second world view, my own, I have followed two approaches: first, to explore my reactions to and understandings of the Blue Pearl narrative; second, to clarify the approach and the potential of transpersonal psychology and to join with others in creating this new form of psychology. Transpersonal psychology suggests at once a new and an ancient vision of reality. It is a psychology that honors all the world's great spiritual traditions and their mythic portrayal and appreciation of the divinity of each human being—the inner Self. Thus, transpersonal psychology extends our sense of the full course of human development to include intuitions of our essential nature and of ways in which that nature might be more fully revealed, realized, and enjoyed.[2]

The term "transpersonal" calls our attention to the largest possible context in which we live and move and have our being. A "transpersonal psychology" would thus be one that comprehends the figural events of our individual lives by remembering, as context, the very ground of existence. Such a psychology would explore not only how the wholeness of humanity, past and present, affects us but also how an unchanging reality, the absolute, manifests in our thoughts and actions. In addition, the term "transpersonal" calls our attention to a state of consciousness that enables some human beings to experience reality in ways that transcend our ordinary "personal" perspectives. Therefore, a transpersonal psychology would also be one that acknowledges the possibility of going beyond the limited outlook of everyday awareness. Such a psychology would be prepared to learn from any persons capable of sharing their evolved state and teaching others how to launch forth on the transformative journey.

If we regard the lives and teachings of the world's great spiritual figures as significant data, then we must reconsider our methodological stance. Transpersonal psychology cannot preserve the objectivity of scientific inquiry and still hope to learn what great teachers have to offer. The effect of the teachers and texts we might study depends in large part upon our willingness to be changed by what we learn. What happens as they teach goes far beyond the transfer of information. We learn by means of our unique responses to first one part and then another of what is being communicated. The research method of transpersonal psychology is thus far from the scientific ideal of detached and interchangeable observers. Rather, it suggests that we maximize our engagement and take careful note of our response, assuming that others will do likewise in relation to other teachers and other texts.

The body of understanding in transpersonal psychology will grow through the efforts of many learners and seekers. As we explore both the uniqueness and the commonalities of our diverse experiences, we will slowly fashion a new vision of human nature and human potential. The result, I am convinced, will provide a much needed corrective to the assumptions and understandings of contemporary psychological thought.

The teachings described in the Blue Pearl narrative and Muktananda's direct, personal interventions have illumined, confronted, and changed my own world view. These changes are reflected in my effort, in the last chapter, to present a more systematic overview of transpersonal psychology. This permits me to discuss some of the features of my current mythic rendering of who I am, who we all are, and what our experience reveals about reality, about how and why we change and in what direction.

I continue to be an academic psychologist and to honor the work and company of my colleagues, whose sturdy, useful world view I carry within me. Although our capacity to contain multiple perspectives and divergent myths is impressive, even if sometimes quite disorienting, an effort to resolve these divergences underlies this book. This effort leads to a recurrent self-inquiry: What would have to change in the psychology I have learned and taught for thirty years if it were to expand to provide a comfortable, even a central place for such notions as the sacred, the absolute, the unmanifest, and the Self? Another question follows: How would I have to change in order to replicate in my own life experience the full course of the transformative process? This book is an attempt to answer these questions. To me, transpersonal psychology is a peculiar and exhilarating arrangement in which each of us can be both researcher and subject, at the same time.

From this perspective, I am impelled to include enough of the primary text, the Blue Pearl narrative, to enable others to form and ponder their own reactions to the transformation of one who has reached the traditional goal of his culture: liberation and final realization of the Self. The central three chapters each present a long selection from Muktananda's narrative. Together, they reveal the evolution of one man's guiding myths through the long and ultimately successful process of inner transformation. His shifting world view focuses our attention on issues we all face in the construction of our own personal and shared myths. We are turned toward exploring the ways in which we view ourselves and those around us and the central images of the ground and cause of all we can ever know.

ACKNOWLEDGMENTS

This book is dedicated to Swami Muktananda. His arrival in Ann Arbor and my subsequent encounters with him fulfilled my longing for a teacher. His life showed me what amazing levels of freedom and joy are humanly possible. The primary text for this study in transpersonal psychology describes his evolving meditative vision of the Blue Pearl. I am deeply grateful that he so graciously permitted me to reprint a series of quotations from his autobiography. His two successors in the Siddha lineage, Swami Chidvilasananda and Swami Nityananda, have been very helpful to this project, and I appreciate their support.

The personal experiences to which I turn throughout the book in an effort to understand the text and my reactions to it are drawn from my involvement, over the past nine years, in Siddha Yoga. Whatever perseverence it has required to keep moving forward in the face of unfamiliar and often confusing events and whatever understanding has emerged from those experiences I attribute in large measure to the great good fortune of having a perfect companion on the journey: my wife, Jean Bisson Mann. The processes of personal transformation that I have come to appreciate over the years have been made real and even delightful by the opportunity to share and observe these changes in the context of our marriage and family. We have learned from each other and from our sons, Larry, Ned, and David, just how immediate and exciting the process of inner development can be. I am particularly grateful for Jean's insightful, comprehending, and helpful responses to the various stages of writing this manuscript.

I have been extremely fortunate to have had fine students and colleagues in my teaching at the University of Michigan. The heads of the Psychology Department, Bill McKeachie, Warren Norman, and Al Cain, and of the Program on Studies in Religion, David Noel Freedman, have been exceptionally kind in their support for this considerable revision in my academic interests. The process of teaching my course, Psychology and Religion, has clarified many things, not the least of which is that, if I stay within certain bounds of appropriateness, I can count on students and colleagues for frank, energetic, and helpful reactions in the service of our common quest for understanding. I attribute much of the pleasure and the learning I have derived from the course to the talented teaching fellows who have worked with me: Deborah Chandler, Harry Cohen, Ali Naqvi, Tony DaSilva, Duke Hill, Barb Branca, Lew Okun, Mike Sayama, Colin Horn, Jan Brink, and Sallie Martin Foley. In the process of working on the Sanskrit text, preparing the Glossary, and writing some technical notes on *yoga* and the Indian spiritual tradition I have had the invaluable assistance of Ahmed Narvil (Devala). My colleague, Madhav Deshpande of the Linguistics Department, has helped me settle on a modified system that provides sufficient, but not excessive, diacritical notations for the Romanized Devanagari script.

A special affection and debt of gratitude is reserved for those who were and are friends no less than teachers, and teachers no less than friends. My vision of the depth and mystery of reality has been profoundly affected by the times spent with friends in whose company doors open and the more limited versions of reality are known to be only temporary. Phil Slater, Merrill Jackson, Perry Hall, Colin Horn, and Shankar and Girija Kruckman (now Swamis Shankarananda and Girijananda) have all played a vital role in the formation of the life tasks reflected in this volume.

My mother, Natalie Cabot Neagle, and my father and step-mother, Richard and Katharine Mann, have consistently affirmed the importance of the process of transformation, through their own lives and in the support they have given me. Each has contributed to my current sense of the unity and integrity of all valid paths of seeking.

ACKNOWLEDGEMENTS

I wish to express my appreciation for funds generously provided for this research in the memory of Helen Dorothy Bailey and for a Faculty Research Grant from the Horace H. Rackham School of Graduate Studies at the University of Michigan.

1 ■

MANY VOICES, ONE VOICE

Swami Muktananda sat on a low couch not more than seven or eight feet from where I sat cross-legged on the floor. I was listening to him talk about the mind and the inner Self beyond the mind. I was only partially attentive, for reasons I will soon make clear, so when the interpreter turned to me as the professor who had helped organize the seminar and asked whether I had any questions, I was somewhat off guard. The question that I managed to ask was, "He says to look within and listen to the inner voice, but what if you hear five or six voices, or even more, all going at once?"

As I listened to the question being translated into Hindi, I agonized inside: "Was that a foolish question? Was it rude? Couldn't I have asked a more dignified, knowledgeable question?" While I was watching the swami's face during the translation, he suddenly smiled a warm, embracing smile and said what was soon conveyed to me as "Yes, yes. But it would still be nice if you could hear that *one* voice."

I sensed a promise in that answer, an affirmation that there is, after all, one voice, and it can be heard. The question didn't seem foolish after all. It seemed, on the contrary, to express the anguish I felt after years of hearing the many voices that represented the inner discord and lack of cohesion among the many parts of myself. Muktananda's response was contained in his smile and the reassurance that it didn't have to be that way.

All that I could figure out then, and over the next few years, was that perhaps the five or six voices would slowly dwindle to four, three, two, and finally one. I wondered which voices would be eliminated and which the eventual winner would be. But the changes that have actually taken place over the past eight years have been more complex than I had expected. To be sure, there are times when I can hear some inner voice with a startling clarity and singularity, but at other times there are still five or six voices, and sometimes more. The most important thing that has happened is that I have slowly stopped perceiving only the apparent differences among the voices, among the various aspects of my own inner world. I have begun to sense that the experience of one voice and the experience of many voices are not mutually exclusive. The many are not engaged in a battle to reduce all but one voice to silence. The many, it turns out, are all versions of the one. All along, the one voice has been speaking *as* the five or six voices; only my preoccupation with their differences has prevented me from detecting their unity.

I can think of no more powerful way to continue this process of inner unification suggested eight years ago by Swami Muktananda than by writing this book. My task is one of honoring the voice of the seeker that I am, the voice of the professor that I am, and the voice of the psychologist that I am. Each of these three voices, and others that will emerge as we go along, has a distinctive way of expressing the one voice that originates from a place beyond labels and aspects. Each seems indispensable to my own exploration and work.

I could probably write about the process of personal exploration and change without reference to my voice as a seeker, my own experience, but that would prevent me from speaking directly and fully about the very essence of what I know. I can sense firm ground under me especially when I am relating the specific events and impressions of my own life.

However, I would be greatly limiting the potential of this exploration if I examined only my own experience. I have selected a thematic excerpt from the autobiography of Swami Muktananda, whose experiences and attainments have come to represent for me the primary teachings about what a human being can attain in a lifetime. In my professorial voice, I shall attempt to clarify the context and import of this text. I will suggest various ways in which the Blue Pearl narrative has "opened up" to me.

Finally, both the narrative and my own direct experience have implications that the psychologist in me cannot ignore. I am convinced that psychology has everything to learn (and nothing to lose) by taking seriously the personal transformation process documented by the Blue Pearl narrative and others like it.

Returning to the scene described in the opening paragraph, how did I happen to be sitting there on the floor? Who was I in those days?

I had never heard of Muktananda before 1974, and in general my attitude toward the various holy men who came to Ann Arbor was fairly negative. I considered them irrelevant to my life, which revolved around teaching, around close interaction with students who were interested in their own self-discovery, growth, and future role in society. I had written about college teaching, and it was my own style that I had in mind when I talked about the teacher as facilitator.

Shortly after my initial meeting with Swami Muktananda, I had a spontaneous visualization that summed up my situation at the time quite well. Late one evening, as I sat by the fire feeling pleasantly drowsy, there appeared in my mind's eye a vivid image. I took the scene to be a New Orleans restaurant—black wrought iron grille-work at the entrance, white tablecloths, and a swiftly moving figure I knew to be me, dressed in white tie and tails. I could see myself flawlessly executing the motions of a maitre d', gliding from table to table: "Is everything all right?" "Is everything all right here?" But as I watched the maitre d' in action, I knew that he/I was hungry to the point of collapse. The same visualization repeated itself on several other occasions. The message was urgent and clear: The facilitator wasn't taking care of himself very well. It was his turn, my turn, to be taken care of, or else.

The emptiness, the hunger, and the urgency were all features of my existence in 1974, but I certainly wasn't morose or unhappy with my life as a teacher. It took certain books that fascinated me to stir some recognition of my situation. I would read about Carlos Castaneda's discovery of his teacher, Don Juan, and ask myself, "Would I be that brave? Hey, when will I learn something really important? Where is my teacher?"

One day, while I was browsing in a bookstore, I noticed an almost indistinct dittoed announcement by Siddha Yoga Dham of Ann Arbor stating that Swami Muktananda was to be in town for two weeks and would be giving a public lecture. In the middle of the flyer was a quote from my former colleague at Harvard, Ram Dass (Richard Alpert), which said how fortunate we in the West were to be visited by a being who was fully evolved. At that point a "message," certainly the first that I would have ever so labeled, hit my consciousness as an almost visible teletype printout of a thought that both was and was not my own: "Well, I guess I'll never get to meet Don Juan." The message surprised me by its eerie sense of being a "received," rather than the usual, seemingly self-initiated, idea. I was convinced that I had to meet this swami and that this was my "cubic centimeter of chance," one of those rare, fateful opportunities that Don Juan alluded to. I promised myself that I would go to Muktananda's lecture toward the end of the month.

However, the timetable I had planned was a little off. Two weeks before the swami was due, the brother of a former graduate student invited me to lunch at Siddha Yoga Dham, accelerating the drama considerably. During lunch I felt on almost totally unfamiliar territory; I tried to make a graceful exit by asking if they had some literature that I could read at home. In fact they did, and so I bought the book *Play of Consciousness*, by Swami Muktananda.

The school term was just starting. I had some free time in the morning, so I started to read the book. The beginning was heavy with references to gods and goddesses. I had long since developed an aversion to all that sort of talk, and I began to look for more interesting sections. Soon I was reading about the author's own experience—his initiation by his guru, his transport into a high state of rapture, and then his nine-year journey through the inner spaces of meditation. These years included various spiritual crises and ended with his "final realization." I recount this plot as if I had read the narrative straight through, but in fact I would often read no more than a page or so and then stop. I would find myself suspended for an hour or more, book open, mind blank, off somewhere in a state that didn't seem anything like sleep.

Muktananda's autobiography revolves around the leitmotiv of the Blue Pearl—a beautiful, shimmering, soft, dazzling meditative vision. Toward the end of the book, he writes that whenever he encounters an individual, he first sees this Blue Pearl, to him an unmistakable sign of that person's innate and essential divinity. Only later does he focus on the individual's specific features and uniqueness. When I read this, a thought, accompanied once again by the eerie sense that it had only partly been authored by the usual me, popped into my head: "Wouldn't it be amazing to stand in front of someone and know that he was seeing your own divinity: a shimmering, blazing Blue Pearl?"

My timetable was still shifting. A week before Muktananda arrived, I got a call from a woman who was in Ann Arbor to make arrangements for his visit. She asked if I would like to convene a brief psychology seminar, like one successfully held at Stanford, during which my colleagues and I could meet Swami Muktananda and discuss the nature of the mind. I didn't want to arrange any such thing, and I couldn't imagine five colleagues who would be even slightly interested. But to my great surprise I agreed to do it. After I had consulted with the woman about the possibility of inviting graduate students to the seminar, the plan began to take shape. It promised to be an interesting occasion.

The day arrived. I was seated directly in front of a small couch, intended for the swami. The room was packed. My wife had come with me, and many old friends from all the years in Ann Arbor were there. As I waited, back came the thought: "Wouldn't it be amazing . . . ?" At that moment Muktananda came in. He sat down, scanned the room for a second, looked right over at me, and gave what seemed to be an unmistakable shake of his head from side to side. My mind computed the meaning in a flash: "Nope! No Blue Pearl! No aura! No nothing! In fact, I have traveled the world over, and you are the first person I have ever met in whom I do not see the Blue Pearl!"

What washed over me then, irresistibly, was the feeling of having received the ultimate rejection. The floor seemed to fall away beneath me. I burned with the sense that I had been scorned, mocked in front of all these people, who certainly must have seen what I had seen. I wondered if I could keep myself from bursting into tears. A sputtering, offended inner voice retaliated: "Who do you think you are? What gives you the right to humiliate me?" But my main reaction was one of utter depression and worthlessness. My worst secret, my emptiness, had been revealed for all to see. I was totally miserable.

Fortunately for me, the story does not end at that point. There I sat, numb with depression, but I noticed, as the swami talked, that the depression was forming or occupying a stratum, as it were, a plainly demarcated layer within what I felt to be my inner reality. There was another stratum present, however, and as my sense of self, my me-ness, drifted toward it, I was overcome by a profound sense of peace, of quiet, of velvet-soft blackness. It was soothing. It was the forest. It was nothing like anything, but it existed, or I existed in it. It seemed to co-exist with that other layer in which the sense of depression and humiliation continued unabated. As I oscillated back and forth between these layers, I felt increasingly removed from any sense of control over, or even responsibility for, my thoughts. The simultaneity of these powerful states and feelings was itself a completely unfamiliar, magical, and amazing experience.

There is a sequel to the story, the denouement which came several days later. I had thought and thought about my encounter with the swami. I could still taste that shocking moment of rejection and its aftermath, but I was beginning to doubt whether I had perceived the situation correctly. His response to me, at least as I had interpreted it, was completely out of line with his response to the many other people he had greeted. I decided to talk with the French psychologist who had spent the previous three years with Muktananda in India. "What does it mean," I asked her, "when he shakes his head like this?" "Oh," she said, laughing, "everyone has trouble with those nonverbal Indian gestures. This gesture," she motioned with her hand, "means 'Come here,' and Westerners think it means 'Goodbye' or 'Get lost!' And that shake of the head means 'Hello. How are you? Welcome.' What did you think it meant?" I didn't tell her, but I clearly had to reconsider the whole encounter: my anticipation, my delight at the prospect of being seen as a Blue Pearl, and my feelings of total rejection. It all led to the question, "If this man hadn't traveled halfway around the world to insult me, if he was not actually the author of that put-down, then who was?"

The entire drama that began with reading about the Blue Pearl and ended with meeting Swami Muktananda was first and foremost a therapeutic intervention in my life and certainly the most powerful confrontation I had ever had. The sequence of events threw open an issue that I had successfully submerged for decades: the issue of self-esteem. Only I could have been the author of that put-down. In all those years of girding myself against excessive self-importance, conceit and arrogance, I had been foolishly inattentive to their opposite. The alleged put-down, as any former analysand should know, was a projection of my own self-deprecation.

In the light of this encounter with Swami Muktananda, it is not surprising that for me the major allure of his Blue Pearl narrative is that it chronicles a radical transformation in self-esteem. It describes how one person came to see his inner nature not as evil or disgusting, not as an emptiness needing to be concealed, but as divine.

By the end of that first meeting with the visiting swami, I was sitting there savoring his affirmation that there was, after all, one voice within. Tears of relief and happiness ran down my face. I felt a hopeless tangle of strong, conflicting emotions and a lingering sense of calm and peace. As I left the room, a reporter from *The Ann Arbor News* stopped me and asked, "What did you think?" I surprised at least myself by answering: "Well, now I know what they mean by the absolute." I doubt that I could have elaborated upon what I had said, but the experience was clear. I had caught hold, in that layer of utter contentedness and peace, of a way of being that was so divergent from any previous mood or moment of my experience that it could only be described by so drastic a term as the absolute. However, I had also glimpsed, in the answer to my question, and in the astoundingly light and self-assured way in which it was given, a person in a state of consciousness so different from anything I had ever known that, again, only a word such as absolute could convey my awe.

Although no words or images can suffice to describe that state, I am nonetheless reminded of a time some years later when I was sitting, courting the state of meditation. A scene in a movie theatre began to unfold before my mind's eye. From the vantage point of "me," the one observing it all, the screen was blocked from view by a long corridor wall. Straight ahead, however, were several rows of movie seats. The brilliant light carrying the images to the screen entered from the right, piercing the dusty air just over the head of the only person I could see in the theatre. The man appeared to be Baba Muktananda. He was watching the screen with enormous delight and yet with a notable serenity. That was the whole of it, just a fragment, but it returns to me now because what I remember best of all is my reaction to the scene. I chose to feel neither envy nor impatience over the fact that the wall prevented me from seeing the screen. On the contrary, I found it reassuring that *someone* could see the screen and enjoy its images. The vignette summarized nicely one outcome of my meeting with Muktananda and my reading of his book. The scene provided me with a brief yet profound glimpse of the state of one who is calmly, firmly, and delightedly in contact with the absolute, and this glimpse constituted a promise that I too could gain that marvelous perspective.

Muktananda's autobiographical account of what he experienced in meditation could create for any or all of us a vantage point similar to mine in the "movie theater" vision. We witness his delight, his serenity, and his capacity to see what we have not yet seen. Isn't this a thoroughly familiar situation? Throughout our lives we have to choose between being discouraged or encouraged by the fact that others apparently can see or know what we cannot. The shaft of light that danced with the shifting images it was carrying to the screen represented, for me, the illuminating Consciousness, the light of the Self that creates all the various forms of thought and awareness. The fact that I had now contacted the figure of a serene teacher with an unobstructed view of this play of forms seemed to bring new goals and new means to my life. It is as if the Blue Pearl narrative, to which I turn now, were Muktananda's answer to my questions, "What do you see? What does it all mean?"

2 ▪

IMAGES OF POWER & PURIFICATION

This exploration in transpersonal psychology is based upon Swami Muktananda's autobiographical account of his evolving experience with the Blue Pearl. In this and the two following chapters I present thematically coherent sections of his narrative.

Three interconnected tasks emerge as we begin to explore the Blue Pearl narrative. They reflect transpersonal psychology's distinctive methods and goals. The first task is to understand the text and its author as if our primary assignment were to learn *from* them and not merely to learn *about* them. With this goal in mind, we can explore Muktananda's cultural context, his purpose in writing this account, and, above all, his experiences and teachings. We stand a far better chance of grasping the meaning of his experiences if we can appreciate how deeply rooted they are in a complex spiritual tradition.

The second task turns us back to ourselves. We need to be aware of how the text connects with our lives. We need to let the narrative stir the memories of parallel experiences. It is important to work not only to clarify the uniqueness of Muktananda's context and symbol system but to build bridges between his account and the understandings we have already developed through our unique life histories. The dual tasks of encountering both the text and ourselves need to proceed in tandem.

The third task involves working with the abstractions of transpersonal psychology, and it requires us to link Muktananda's account with not only our private experience but with the central concepts of the great spiritual traditions of the world. The commonly reported occurrences and understandings are a source of insight as we explore the unfamiliar territory of Muktananda's narrative. And, equally, the more we understand the text and ourselves, the more we can contribute to the development of a useful and complete vision of reality. Analysis of text is thus an invitation to understand another human being whose account is itself a teaching. It is an invitation to self-exploration and discovery. And it is the mode by which transpersonal psychology offers and receives insight into human transformation. Let us begin with the first of these tasks.

Muktananda's Life and Culture

Swami Muktananda was born in the south of India, in Mangalore to be exact, in 1908. He was thirty-nine at the time he received initiation from his guru, Bhagavan Nityananda. The meditation experiences he recounts in *Play of Consciousness* took place over the nine years following his initiation. He wrote the book in three weeks' time at the age of sixty-one. He died, or, as the Indians would put it, "left his body," in 1982 at seventy-four.

Muktananda was fifteen when he met the immensely powerful and well-known saint, Nityananda, who wandered freely throughout India before eventually settling near Bombay, in Ganeshpuri. The meeting, Muktananda says, so affected him that he resolved to pursue the spiritual path, and within a year he had left home to become a *sādhu*, a seeker. He wandered, homeless with few possessions, over much of India for the next twenty-five years. During his early twenties he took the vows of the *sannyāsin* and became a swami, or monk, in the Saraswati order. Over the years he became proficient in Indian medicine, cooking, and horticulture and well versed in both the scriptures and the writings of the Indian poet-saints.

By his late thirties, Muktananda was considered by many to be their teacher or guru. He considered himself, however, to be "incomplete," still not fully in possession of the great, final attainments of the spiritual quest. At the urging of one of his long-time spiritual guides, he went to Ganeshpuri and was soon united with Nityananda in the bond of guru and disciple. He received initiation by *shaktipāt*, meaning literally "the descent of grace," and began to experience the longed-for fruits of his seeking. At his guru's instruction, he returned to an essentially solitary life of meditation and other spiritual practices for the next nine years. Covering this nine-year period, *Play of Consciousness* is a story of what in the Indian tradition would be called a completed *sādhanā*, or journey, to final realization. This attainment was joyfully proclaimed by Nityananda in 1956. But the journey was by no means a smooth and easy one.

Play of Consciousness serves as a teacher's message to spiritual seekers. It is clear that Muktananda was unprepared for some of his crucial experiences during the nine-year period of intense *sādhanā*. Only through the opportune guidance of several teacher-friends and his gradual discovery of key spiritual texts was he able to accept and understand his experiences. Hence, one function of his autobiography is to reassure and encourage those who are blocked, as he himself had been, by fear, confusion, and doubt.

Finally, it is important to know that, in the context of his own culture, Swami Muktananda was a traditional teacher. He was not preoccupied with innovating or with revising existing teachings. He was perfectly content to continue the long chain of guru-disciple relationships. To most of us, however, his teachings are a combination of unfamiliar elements. Here, very briefly enumerated, are a few of these elements as they emerge in the autobiography:

1. There is the central paradox of a Supreme Reality that is formless, unknowable, and transcendent (sometimes called the Shiva aspect) and that *simultaneously* manifests in and as the world of form, sporting as conscious energy (sometimes called the Shakti aspect).

2. Direct experience of that Supreme Reality, in this lifetime, in this body, is of crucial importance, as is the pursuit of the self-evident truths that manifest uniquely and appropriately in each seeker, leading ultimately to the ineffable experience called final realization of the Self.

Thus, Muktananda's tradition is not dominated by any religious dogma or ritual. In fact, like other teachers such as Ramakrishna Paramahamsa and Sai Baba of Shirdi, Muktananda embraces many Islamic, especially Sufi, and non-Vedic Indian writings.

3. His tradition is not one that encourages asceticism, a turning away from the world, or the deliberate practice of "supernatural" powers. These practices tend to block one's devotion and one's appreciation of and reliance on grace. Muktananda emphasizes a life-affirming, joyful engagement in a radical process of transformation that encompasses rather than shuns every aspect of life.

4. The Upanishads and Kashmir Shaivite texts of 900–1300 A.D., which Muktananda often cites, locate the goal and experiential process of *sādhanā* in the context of a nondualistic conception of reality. Kashmir Shaivism, though not very different from Shankarāchārya's Advaita Vedānta, is more closely attuned to the imagery and evidence of Muktananda's experience. The heart of the nondualistic schools of Indian philosophy is found in the assertion that no final, irresolvable difference exists between God and the individual human being, between God's transcendent and immanent aspects, or between our daily life experiences and that of heaven on earth.

5. The process of transforming any verbal formulas into real understanding requires intervention. This intervention occurs so freely and unconditionally that it is experienced by the seeker as grace. The equation has no terms referring to the seeker's insistence or cleverness, although self-effort is sometimes viewed as important. The source of this grace is sometimes called the Lord or the Goddess and sometimes the guru, the human agent who can initiate, guide, and confirm the completion of this difficult process. One key element of the nondualistic approach is that no ultimate distinction is made between God, the guru, and the Self of the seeker who has undertaken this transformative journey.

The Blue Pearl Narrative

In selecting the passages that follow, I adopted broad criteria for determining relevance, including references not only to the Blue Pearl but to related visionary phenomena, the blue light of consciousness and the blue star. I included, as well, experiences that clarify the context and precursors of the Blue Pearl vision. These excerpts would certainly make even more sense in the light of the entire autobiography. My intention, however, is merely to show the development of one central image—the Blue Pearl—in the climactic stages of one man's spiritual evolution. With that purpose in mind, let us explore the narrative, beginning with the account of the Blue Pearl's first appearance in the author's meditative experiences.

> My eyeballs had been revolving, and now the pupils were centered and had become as one. The eyeballs rolled up and down. Then, while this was happening, a tiny, extremely brilliant dot shot out of my eyes with the speed of lightning and then went back in again. This is a secret, mysterious, and marvelous process. In an instant the tiny blue dot illuminated everything in every direction. If I were sitting facing east, the whole of the east would be lit up. If I were facing south, the whole of the south would be lit up.
>
> Siddha students, how can I tell you about the greatness and glory of that Blue Pearl! It was animated, and faster than a flash of lightning. When I saw it, I was filled with many emotions. Would Rama or Krishna or my especially adored Parashiva come with it? Who was I to meet after Airavata? I was greedy for visions, but still my mind was happy and full of joy and contentment. My days passed differently from before, for my heart was deeply satisfied with the vision of the Blue Pearl, and it told me that I had been blessed with a gift from the Goddess Kundalini. I began to honor everyone in my heart.
>
> When my eyes stopped rolling, they would stay turned upward. I would keep looking upward, and if I looked down it would hurt. Sometimes my eyes stayed open without blinking. I started to feel a pain between the eyebrows, which was so strong that I could not sleep at night. Then a light came in meditation, like a candle flame without a wick, and stood motionless in the *ajna chakra,* the two-petaled lotus between the eyebrows. It was extremely brilliant and beautiful. As I gazed at it, quite forgetful of myself, my vision became blurred. Next to that light is the path that the awakened Kundalini takes on Her way to the *sahasrara.* This is the pathway of the Siddhas, which does not open without the full grace of a Guru. No matter how great your devotion or your *tapasya,*

no matter how much you meditate or how many *kriyas* you experience, this path is very difficult to open without the Guru's grace. There is only one way: *gurukripā hi kevalam gurorājnā hi sādhanam*—"The Guru's grace is the only way, the Guru's command is the only method."

This *chakra* was also pierced, and the *pranashakti* began to climb higher. I saw the wickless flame constantly before me and was constantly filled with bliss. The place of the flame is the same place where devout Indian women put *kumkum* every day as a symbol of their fidelity in marriage. They put *kumkum* there in the name of their husbands or just because it is customary, but that place is actually the seat of the Guru, and it is there that the presiding deity of the Guru's seat lives, in the form of the two seed syllables *"ham"* and *"ksham."* We owe our existence to it. The flame is one form of the supreme Self. Times have changed now, and some women have forgotten this duty. Everything is becoming the opposite of what it once was.

I kept seeing this divine flame, and as I contemplated it, other forms would appear within it, each form within the previous one: first the red aura, then the white flame, then the black light, and finally the Blue Pearl. As I passed through all these different stages, moving ahead, my joy and ecstasy kept increasing.

I was beginning to experience a new kind of bliss. I had frequent visions, which were absolutely authentic. When I saw the Blue Pearl, the condition of my body and mind, and my way of understanding, began to change. I felt more and more delight in myself, and was filled with pure and noble feelings. I started to tire of all forms of external associations and became addicted only to meditation. I always asked myself, "What shall I see today?" This was the only thing I waited for, the only thing I took interest in, the only thing I enjoyed, and it became my daily action and my daily meditation. [Pp. 127–129]

I did not meditate out of fear, but with enthusiasm and faith and love. I did not meditate to please anyone or to get any benefits from anyone or to satisfy a desire, sensual or otherwise. I did not meditate to rid myself of any illness,

> physical or mental, nor to gain fame through the miraculous and supernatural powers I might acquire. No one forced me to meditate. I did not meditate because religion says that it is good to meditate. I meditated solely for the love of God, because I was irresistibly drawn toward the Goddess Chiti Shakti, and to explore my own true nature.
>
> As soon as I sat, I passed into meditation. The presiding deity of each sense organ would come and stand before me. I would see a very special kind of light made up of many colors flashing through the 72,000 *nadis* like lightning. Then would come the red, white, and black lights, and, for a second, the Blue Light. These lights appeared one within the other, the smaller within the larger, the one being the subtle cause and also the support of the other. [P. 130]

Through his account of these vivid, meditative experiences Muktananda introduces what he later called "the main topic" of his autobiography, the vision of the Blue Pearl.[1] How can I, trained most of my life in psychology's way of explaining (away) such experiences, begin to contact the meaning of the Blue Pearl experiences?

Images of the Sacred

One place to start is with the polarity that underlies this and all such visionary experiences: the polarity between the ordinary and the sacred. Against the backdrop of ordinary thoughts and everyday life, there emerges a series of internal, visual, highly charged representations of the non-ordinary. This breakthrough of the divine, or breakthrough into the divine, is what strikes me first about the event. It is the moment of theophany, revelation, discontinuity. For Muktananda the occasion was set within the formal practice of meditation, but we all have access to these moments of breakthrough, whether waking or asleep, at home or by the sea.

We go along, leading our lives, and suddenly the ordinary world becomes charged, numinous, startlingly beautiful, compelling, or soft. Some previously unacknowledged truth or splendor emerges and becomes something that we know—and know that we know.

But what do we mean by a sacred realm? Is the ordinary, profane world like Dorothy's Kansas and the sacred world like the

Kingdom of Oz? Is it out there, somewhere else, wholly other? Is a sudden encounter with the sacred like discovering a waterfall in the middle of unexplored territory? Is the transformation process then a matter of learning how to get there and back? Is the sacred an independent plane of existence that awaits us mortals? Or is the sacred always here, unacknowledged, in our latent understandings? If so, then the notion of "discovering" the sacred is not a very accurate rendering of the process; rather, our lives might better be seen as efforts to reduce the tendency of one layer of consciousness (the ordinary or profane) to obliterate all other layers. Is the sacred active, purposeful, striving to be represented in our awareness? If so, then our manifest awareness might reflect a constantly shifting mixture of images that derive from the many layers of consciousness. And if that is so, then perhaps we can deliberately maximize those emergent images that resonate with and convey the sacred already within us. The Blue Pearl narrative attests to the effectiveness of two age-old ways of producing exactly this maximization.

It suggests that, if we really wanted to experience more fully the latent or sacred world view, then we could choose, as Muktananda did, to come into as close contact as possible with a human being whose awareness is dominated by the sense of the sacred. In traditional terms, we could seek the company of a saint; we could find our teacher. The narrative also suggests that once the process of transformation was under way we could also practice meditation, as Muktananda did. The simple act of turning away from the world of the senses, away from ordinary memories and worries, and turning toward our deeper layers invites, as Muktananda might put it, the Self to shine forth.

As Muktananda carries out the command of his guru to go off by himself and meditate, what happens? The process of sensing the sacred in more and more of his experience accelerates. It slows in the face of fears and obstacles, but these are surmounted and the process moves ahead. What does this mean to us? How can we use Muktananda's experience to facilitate that very process in ourselves?

When all the details of the narrative have been cleared away, I am left with several major implications of his experience for my understanding of our common reality as human beings. We are constantly being spoken to by our own deepest, sacred Self. The language of the Self is not always one of words, but sometimes it is. Sometimes it speaks in the familiar mythic, numinous symbolism of a cultural tradition; sometimes its symbols are virtually universal in their power to affect us. The Self is shining forth and, in its range of expression and communication within our conscious awareness, it is bedazzling. We receive intimations of the sacred realm of our own being whenever we are closely attuned to our inner screen, as in dreaming, meditation, and contemplation, or to the outer screen, as in experiencing nature, entering a cathedral, approaching a great being, or seeing someone we love.

The images and symbols of the sacred we find in Muktananda's wide-ranging meditative experiences leap beyond the bounds of a particular culture. Of these, four recurrent and, I suspect, universal images remind me of my own inner symbol system and its efforts to convey the latent understanding of the Self. Each of these images of the sacred is conveyed by the Blue Pearl.

The first image is of the Center. We drift through life, and the ordinary world we inhabit is the world of, at the very least, the "ten thousand things." Each fragmented, clamorous detail bobs up and down in a sea of other details, events, and qualities. Sometimes, however, this chaos yields, and a structure emerges. More fundamental categories replace our arbitrary array of labels. We sense that more powerful causes are operating behind the seemingly random nature of events. From our frantic role-playing selves, often redefined by each new situational demand, more and more comprehensive identities begin to evolve. The end of this wonderful process is the experience of "the still point of the turning world," the *bindu*, the Blue Pearl.[2] As we approach the Center, everything becomes more subtle, more powerful, more the pure expression of the one inner Self. The Blue Pearl is both expression of the Self and proof of its attainment. Muktananda generates the message from one layer of his being as symbol and receives it at another layer as grace, as revelation. The Blue Pearl, standing at the Center, is one primary and complete symbolic expression of the Self.

The second image of the sacred is completely consonant with the first, but its impact on us may differ. The sacred Essence, uniformly present in and as everything, is but another way that we represent to our conscious awareness our latent understanding of the

Self. We are lifted from the relative world and propelled by this image into the world of the absolute, the Ground of all, the world of final equality, where "everything is . . . *x*." What words or phrases do we use for *x*? Truth, God's creation, alive, love itself, energy, consciousness, filled with light, beautiful, good, real, the one Self, and on and on. The blue light of Consciousness is in everything, manifesting as everything. So, too, in the countless experiences of cosmic consciousness, an image of the sacred appears as the One in everything, bursting forth. A similar representation of our latent understanding is also effected in such formulations as the seamless (but definitely not empty) Void.

The third image of the sacred is the unbounded and undifferentiated Whole. The Blue Pearl emerges as not *a* thing, but as *everything*. The Center and the seamless Whole, which is infused with the one Essence, are not divergent images but one complex expression of the nature of the Self. The paradox of the sacred as both Center and Whole recurs regularly in many cultures, East and West.

The fourth image of the sacred conveys the dynamic, purposive aspect of the Self. One way to represent the intentionality of the sacred is to imagine a recognizably human figure as the embodiment of the Self. From our depths comes the powerful, evocative image of the Sacred Person: the Goddess, the Lord, the Redeemer, or the Guru. This image captures the primacy and the benevolent purpose of the Sacred Person. In the relationship that expresses our response, we feel we are the child, the creature. We feel gratitude and love for the grace we have received. The Blue Pearl narrative is a hymn of praise to the One that manifested through Muktananda's transforming experiences. Muktananda, in an early passage of praise and worship of the Goddess, Mother Kundalinī, calls the Blue Pearl Her "vehicle" and attributes the vision of it to Her intentional manifestation, as blessing and guidance.[3] However, the Person and the Self are not two separate entities. As Muktananda learned, it is our own Self that is being revealed whether we sense that Person in meditation, in the sacred grove, or at the feet of the guru. Our experience is being caused, as it were, not by some separate external force but by the inner latent truth that takes the form of our apperceived reality.

Visions Leading up to the Blue Pearl

To expand our exploration of the meaning of the Blue Pearl vision, we can also look at the sequence of events preceding it. Muktananda states that the Blue Pearl emerged after a prolonged period of meditation, during which a number of significant developments took place. The blue light that eventually gave way to the Blue Pearl was preceded by meditations in which a red aura predominated, then by visions of a thumb-sized white flame, and then by a small black light the size of a finger-tip. Each light, smaller than its predecessor, would be accompanied by a sense of deepened meditation and intensification of involuntary physical movements, called *kriyās*. Here, Muktananda describes an important aspect of the period just prior to the Blue Pearl's emergence:

> Next, the pupils of both my eyes became centered together. I began to see one thing with two eyes. In the scriptures this is called *bindu bheda*. After this had happened, a blue light arose in my eyes. This is the necessary preliminary to the *shambhavi mudra*. When the aspirant experiences the *neelodaya*, the dawning of the blue light, it signifies the dawning of his supreme good fortune. When the process starts, some aspirants fear that they may lose their eyesight. With me, my eyes rolled so violently around and around and up and down that it seemed as if they would fall out. Some people saw it happening and they too were frightened. But I put all my trust in the Goddess, believing that it is not I, but She, the Paramatmashakti, the power of God who is within us, who does everything. And so all my fears vanished.
>
> As the eyes revolve, the optical *chakras* are pierced, which pleases their deity. Sadhakas should not forget that each one of our senses has its particular deity. While the *chakras* are still unpurified, the deity carries on its work in the ordinary way, but when the *chakras* are purified they become invested with divine powers. When the optical *chakras* are purified by piercing, their deity bestows divine sight on the aspirant, and he becomes clairvoyant.

> Now in meditation I felt bliss and also a growing energy. At the same time, the pain in my eyes, ears, and the space between the eyebrows increased. My meditation would be centered first on the red aura, then on the white flame, and then on the black light. When I sat for meditation, I would have some bodily *kriyas*, then the *prana* would flow forcefully through my *nadis*, and my tongue would curl back into the *khechari mudra*; my meditation would then become perfectly steady. I would feel waves of ecstasy welling up inside me. But even though I was completely carried away, I understood everything that was happening around me, and my understanding has not changed in the least today. It is as it was then. Such understanding is very important. Sometimes I felt that my ability to understand was also new, because I remembered even the tiniest details of my experiences. I remained very attentive and tried to understand this power of intuitive intelligence. [Pp. 125–126]

This short passage points to several important elements in the narrator's spiritual development. First, there is the process of purification, seen as a necessary condition for the aspirant's progress. One vivid sign and effective means of this process is the *kriyā*. Muktananda's eyes were rolling around, up and down, painfully, even dangerously, in the opinion of some onlookers. However, the crucial attribution that Muktananda makes is to understand all these events as being under the control of the benevolent, all-powerful Goddess. Far from being a torment, they were experienced as a blessing, a sign of supreme good fortune. He saw them as quickening the tempo of his spiritual evolution, under the benign guidance of the divine energy he worshipped as Kundalinī.

Three Paths of Spiritual Seeking

The farther we go in exploring Muktananda's early experiences with the Blue Pearl, the more compelling it is to see them as expressing a common concern with the theme of power and purification. And the clearer this becomes, the more it becomes possible to see the early phase of Muktananda's journey as following one of several possible paths. We have something to gain from stepping back for a moment to sketch out the additional themes which have yet to emerge in their fullest form. We can understand the meaning of these experiences better if we can appreciate the contrast that sets them apart from later phases and divergent paths of spirituality.

In the Indian tradition the three major forms of spiritual seeking are often differentiated as the path of power and purification (*yoga*), the path of devotion (*bhakti*), and the path of understanding (*jnāna*). What complicates matters is that there are narrow and broad definitions of the term *yoga*. The narrow definition, which I follow in contrasting *yoga* with other paths, is best exemplified by Eliade's discussion of *yoga* as "any *ascetic technique* and any *method of meditation*" that is directed toward "gaining liberation."[4] This form of spiritual seeking I refer to as the path of purification. The broader definition of *yoga* leans on the Sanskrit root *yuj*, "to bind together," and thus permits consideration of other modes of attaining union with the absolute. In that broader sense, then, one can speak of *bhakti yoga* or *jnāna yoga*, since devotion and understanding, no less than ascetic purification, can lead to union or liberation. In my analysis of the text, however, the unmodified term, *yoga*, and derivative terms such as *yogī* (one who practices *yoga*) are used in their narrow sense, as but one of several paths distinguished in Indian spiritual life.

How useful are these categories in analyzing a complex personal account such as the Blue Pearl narrative? How are these paths related to one another: as steps on a ladder, as paths leading up the same mountain, converging only at the top, as themes that are equally necessary throughout one's development for a full, balanced, and successful journey? Or are they essentially the same, differing only superficially?

At what level of analysis shall we work to understand these three paths? My approach derives from the thesis that each of the apparently divergent paths, the path of purification, of devotion, and of understanding, can be distinguished by how it answers three basic questions posed by the spiritual seeker: Who am I? Who (or what) is the Other? What is the relationship between this I and that Other?

In the classical Indian tradition of *yoga*, especially the system associated with Patanjali, the question "Who am I?" is answered by a contingency: It all depends on your effort to disentangle yourself from the ignorance of ordinary consciousness and the weakness or impurity of your ordinary psychophysiological instrument—your mind and gross physical body. It all depends on your attainment, by means of the ecstatic, thought-free state (*samādhi*), of liberation (*moksha*) and your ability to proclaim, as a liberated soul (*jīvanmukta*), "I am the free, unbound Spirit." The hallmark of the yogic path is technique, in fact a whole set of interlocking techniques: intense concentration on one point (*ekāgratā*), asceticism (*tapas*), and purificatory and strengthening exercises (*āsana* and *prāṇāyāma*), to name only some. This is a path in which the will of the seeker is put to the test. Under the direction of a teacher, the seeker gradually acquires the power necessary to overcome the ordinary state of body and mind, with its seemingly inescapable qualities of pain and evil, birth and death. The traditional yogic path is considered to be an extremely difficult, demanding one that requires great courage, strength, and endurance. At one extreme of this path, the stance taken in relation to the sacred is heroic; this is the path of taking heaven by storm. Thus, the answer to the question "Who am I?" emphasizes one's attainments and progress, upon which depends the very quality of one's life.

What about the Other? References in classical yogic systems to any God figure are rather subdued. Initially, at least, the *purusha*, the inner Self, which ordinary consciousness tends to obscure, has the feel of Otherness. Even in the oldest forms of *yoga*, there is a sense of the Other as the one who helps and protects: Ishwara is the Other, not only as the primal creator but also as the source of that power without which the entire creation would falter and fail. In later forms, and in the somewhat analogous paths of shamanism, the Other becomes even more concrete. The source of all power is sometimes seen to be retentive, jealous, testing the would-be recipient to determine his worthiness and motivation.

Hence, the relationship between the seeker and the Other in the path of the will may resemble that of two adversaries, with the more powerful exacting extraordinary feats of precision in ritual or endurance in austerity. Particularly impressive acts of self-control and endurance seem to "force the hand" of the god, obliging him to grant some boon, and yet the situation is usually more complex. One gains power from the Other, but only by a radical surrendering of one's ordinary self. This in turn leads to the more profound state of merging one's own will with the will or power of the Other. The boundaries begin to collapse, but duality tends to remain; it is as if even the liberated person were, despite the experience of freedom, still functioning in relation to the supreme Other as its vessel or representative on this plane.

The excerpts from the Blue Pearl narrative in this chapter are filled with the imagery and experience of the yogic path: visions of lights, spontaneous physical movements, a series of changes in the physical body, and psychic abilities, to list but a few examples. This section is far more dominated than the two following chapters by themes of energy, power, endurance, and will.

Turning next to the path of the heart, we can expect to find very different answers to the fundamental questions. If power is the primary means of the path of the will, then love is obviously primary in the path of devotion. Who am I? I am the devotee, the seeker, the creature who stands in relation to the supreme Other, the Lord, the Creator and Sustainer of worldly existence. The contrasting feelings that one may experience on this path are (1) union or closeness versus separation, loss of contact, distance; (2) a sense of being loved, protected, guided versus a sense of being punished, rejected, despised by the Other. Both are evident, for example, in traditional Judeo-Christian imagery. Sometimes one experiences both the presence and warmth of God, as in certain tender scriptural scenes. Sometimes one experiences God's presence only through "the terrible wrath." Sometimes there is only the immense silence of the *deus otiosus*, the far distant God; this may be seen either as the ultimate punishment or merely as evidence of a weakened or inattentive deity.

On the path of the heart the key attributes of a seeker include devotion, openness, remembrance and attentiveness, obedience, and surrender. The devotee is enjoined not so much to perform some effective, powerful action as to create the favorable conditions under which the Other may initiate what is usually called an act of grace. The devotee is enjoined to avoid actions that may close the heart, cause inattention, or make the devotee less available to the Other. The primary actor is not the heroic *yogī* (the "I"), but the Lord, the guru, or the Goddess (the Other).

In all of this the question of the relationship between the devotee and the Other is paramount. It is an evolving, conditional relationship, full of positive and negative contingencies. Seekers and communities preserve careful records concerning the lives of those who serve as positive or negative examples, lives that give evidence as to what leads to what in this encounter with the Other.

In the Indian spiritual tradition one moment or act that epitomizes the path of the heart is called *darshan*. The term literally means "the act of seeing a saint or idol"; its full connotation is that the Other has manifested and the devotee has had the eyes to see. This occurrence is both a culmination and a transformation in the spiritual life of the devotee. *Darshan* does come in response to yearning and to readiness, but, again, no effort is thought to be sufficient, only to be necessary. It is one of the simplest and most powerful manifestations of divine grace, the greatest fortune; its effects are every bit as important as its unknowable cause. One effect is to dispel doubt and to awaken or implant a sense of having been blessed. Thereafter, the entire world is always, if one can sustain the memory of such a moment, connected to the sacred realm, always in some way a continuing moment of *darshan*. In this new state, the devotee is full of the sense of connection, participation in the divine, openness, and love. His answer to the question "Who am I?" is transformed accordingly.

A fine example of the consummation of the path of devotion can be found in the next chapter. Muktananda describes the *darshan* of the Lord, the Blue Person emerging from the Blue Pearl.

The third path, that of *jnāna*, or understanding, is quite distinct from the path of the will or the heart. This is the path of the pure intellect, which, at least from the time of Aristotle through Thomas Aquinas, was taken to be a function sharply differentiated from reason or thinking. It comes closer to what we might now call intuition or direct knowledge, as Bergson and Jung discuss it. In the Indian analysis of the fourfold psychic instrument, this function is performed by the *buddhi*. Its noblest task is to discriminate between the illusory and the eternal and thus to provide an opening to the light of the Self. In any case, to call this the path of understanding is not meant to glorify precisely what this path is trying to go beyond: the mind and its discursive, rational, logical thinking. In both Eastern and Western traditions, although the mind has been honored for its necessary role in dealing with the ordinary world of sense objects, ideas, and their logical relations, it has been deemed incapable of probing the realm of the sacred or the Spirit.

The path of *jnāna* is a path that values direct experience of the unity of all things—an apprehension of the One, the Real, the Eternal behind and/or within the many, the apparent, and the transitory. The vivid imagery of the paths of the will and the heart is notable for its capacity to evoke appropriate resolve and right relations, but the imagery of this path always seems to be aiming at some inexpressible paradox: the One in the many but also the many in the One; the inexorable unfolding of the process of cause and effect, but also the timeless simultaneity of the unconditioned unity.

As Schurmann suggests in his analysis of Meister Eckhart, a Western sage and Dominican monk of the fourteenth century, the sense of separation can yield and be replaced by the radical intuition that there is an identity between, a common origin of, man and God.[5] Meister Eckhart calls the common origin the Godhead, and Jung and several other twentieth century writers build upon his understanding that God, man, and the world have equal status in the diverse outpouring of the One. In the Indian tradition the same understanding produces the four *mahāvākya*s, or proclamations, which include the highest teaching of the Upanishads: "That which is the finest essence, this whole world has that as its *ātman*. That is reality. That is Atman. That art thou, Svetaketu."[6] Direct experience of the ground of all existence, the Self of all, leads to a unique answer to the second question posed at the outset: "There is no Other. There is only the One, the perfect, the single principle manifesting in and as everything." If that is so, how can one answer the first question "Who am I?" other than by some intuitive affirmation such as, "I am That!"

The gradual inclusion and annihilation of all boundaries and distinctions within one vibrant, joyful universal category is characteristic of the path of understanding. The third section of the narrative, presented in chapter four, is remarkable for its ability to convey this intuition, again through the imagery and experience of the Blue Pearl.

Yogic Experiences

After examining how the three basic questions of the seeker are answered by each of the three paths, I will return to the very important question of how they fit together. Now, we turn to the first occurrence of the Blue Pearl and the subsequent visions, examining them in the context of a yogic *sādhanā*.[7] The guiding hand of the Other is understood to be the basis of the purificatory transformation that is taking place spontaneously. The same benign Other is understood to be the source of the numerous blessings, some in the form of sublime visions, others in the form of ecstatic movements of the body (*mudrā*s). The received knowledge of yogic anatomy, with its four bodies, subtle channels and *chakra*s, Muktananda now takes to be completely valid. His meditative visions locate them as true of his own body; they have become his own undeniable experience.[8] The following excerpt describes a similar validation of the yogic perspective:

> My body was now very thin, but full of energy. I was still meditating. I had completed the meditation on Krishneshwari, the black light, and was now meditating more and more on Neeleshwari, the Blue Pearl. The black light stands for the causal body, which Jnaneshwar Maharaj called *parvardha*—"the tip of the finger." Its seat is in the heart, and in this body deep and dreamless sleep occurs. It is the pure unstained state beyond the senses, and in this state there are no desires, but only the enjoyment of bliss. The individual soul in this body is represented by the *"m"* in *Aum* and is called *prajna*.
>
> Through meditation it is possible to have direct experience of the gross, subtle, causal, and supracausal bodies. The causal body, which I have named Krishneshwari, the black goddess, and which I experienced as the size of a fingertip, is the third petal of the lotus of the four bodies. The first petal is red, the second white, and the third black. Oh Siddha students, you may experience all this for yourselves in meditation. This is something which can be attained only through the regular practice of yoga. The saints have called this *devayana pantha*—"the way of the gods." Kundalini Yoga is the great yoga and the way of God revealed, because in this yoga there is no difference between ordinary life, spiritual life, and

God. It is called Siddha Marga, the path of perfection. It is the path to liberation.

The blue *akasha*, an expansion of blue color, began to appear in meditation and with it, the *neela bindu*, the Pearl of infinite power. As I watched it, I felt as if my eyes were going to burst. My eyelids would not move; I could not open or close my eyes. I was completely entranced by the *bindu*. I saw a new light outside also, and as I passed into meditation, Kundalini Mahamaya would appear before me in many different forms. Whatever form She took, I regarded in the same way—as the supreme Shakti, the Goddess Chiti. The Blue Light came and went, came and went. My eyes rolled up so that they were a little above the eyebrows, and apparently lost. Something important was happening in the cranial region. There are some *chakras* there, and this process was happening to purify them. [Pp. 134–135]

Now my meditation went beyond the black light to the Blue Pearl. As soon as I sat down to meditate, there would be gentle movement in my body and then a rush of new energy through the *nadis*. The red, white, black, and Blue lights would come. My meditation would stabilize itself, and sometimes I would pass into a deep *tandra* trance and would travel to other worlds. I saw everything while sitting in my hut. Every day I had some new experience. My body was becoming light, slim, agile, healthy, and strong. I could see the central *nadi*, the *sushumna*, which is silver-colored and tinged with gold. It stands like a pillar, and all the *nadis* receive vibrations of power from it. When a sadhaka is meditating, he sometimes feels a pain in the *muladhara*, at the base of the spine, which is due to the transmission of Shakti from the *sushumna* into the other *nadis*. Sometimes I would have a new movement in the heart, in which an egg-shaped ball of radiance would come into view. This is the vision of the radiant thumb-sized Being, who is described as follows in the *Shvetashvatara Upanishad: angusthamatrah puruso'ntaratma sada jananam hridaye sannivistah*—"The inner soul always dwells in the heart of all men as a thumb-sized being." [P. 136]

The unfolding drama of the Blue Pearl visions is certainly not a random assembly of isolated vignettes. There is an emergent form that contains these experiences and reveals a gradual but momentous developmental sequence. How can we detect and appreciate the cumulative import of these evolving images?

Intuitions of the Light

Any statements concerning the sacred, the Goddess, or the Self are best treated as intuitions: that is, unprovable, not necessarily logical, and profoundly personal expressions of one's shifting inner reality. Their value lies in their capacity to articulate, however incompletely, the meaning that is forming beneath, or perhaps beyond, the level of conscious, rational, or verbalized thought. This value is derived from both the poet's love of giving form to the inchoate and the teacher's love of providing others with some hint or technique that points them toward their own deepest understandings. The entire narrative expresses for Muktananda, and attempts to invoke for the reader, what I consider to be five central and interconnected intuitions. They are not the only intuitions one can find in the text—I offer this framework only as a pattern that recurs with shifting emphasis throughout the narrative and the autobiography from which it is drawn.

If I may adopt one virtually universal symbol of the sacred or the absolute, the image of light, or the light, then the five intuitions form the following sequence:

1. There is light.
2. I see the light.
3. The light sees me.
4. The light is in me.
5. I am the light.

Let us elaborate on each of these.

1. **There is light**. It exists. This intuition is counterposed to the familiar conclusion that there is no light, that perhaps there never was light, or that it has become so feeble and remote that it no longer plays any role in our lives. These familiar and somewhat forlorn conclusions gain and diminish in their hold on us. It is no wonder that the intuition asserting the existence of light is so often compared

to an ember: It can be all but extinguished and then suddenly flare up, after years of denial, with even a moment's fueling from some confirmatory experience. To say that the light exists is to throw the world of shadow and relativity, the world of "Is this all there is?" into stark contrast with another world, the world of "No, this isn't all there is. There's more."

2. **I see the light.** To expand from the intuition "There is light (but I can't see it)" to "I see the light" is to have one's intuitions deepened and stabilized by direct experience. The issue shifts from "How do I know? On faith? From the evidence of someone else's experience?" to "How steadily and with what intensity does my experience confirm my sense of seeing the light?" It is one thing to encounter a teacher who says, "Believe me. It's true." It is another to see the light pouring out of him or to find one's moments of prayer in his presence filled with the same brilliance. Even a glimpse of that glory may be enough to change one's life completely.

3. **The light sees me**. "I am seen. I am known, loved, protected." We conjure up images of gentle rain falling from heaven or of the sun spreading its warmth equally on weed and crop. Suddenly it is not only that I glimpse the light. Now I perceive the light as fully endowed with intention and agency. My sense of agency or doership is rearranged, and, as the experience of being the receiver deepens, the word "grace" takes on new meaning and relevance. There is light, and there is a palpable relationship between it and me. Even if I do not consciously see the light, I may still sense the light, filling the darkness and overcoming my blindness.

4. **The light is in me**. The light and the eternal spirit are not so wholly "other" that one should imagine them residing in some inaccessible place and time. They are here, now, within. Our notions of a soul or a spark of God's flame residing within this body represent our efforts to localize the light. There is some inner Other, and, just as in the Gnostic fable about the lost pearl of great price, it can be rediscovered, much to our delight. There is, in this intuition, an appreciation of the intimacy that exists between us and our inner divinity. There may be moments of inaccessibility, as if some inner passageway were clogged by desire, pride, or ignorance, but the light is still there, enduring the dark night of the soul.

5. **I am the light**. Suddenly the last barrier is down. The light exists as me. All dualistic constructions of reality seem irrelevant. There is no Other, inner or outer. "I am That," *so'ham*, arises as the verbal approximation of some vast understanding. I am the light.

In the visionary drama of the Blue Pearl narrative, we see how these five intuitions (and others) take shape and become irreversibly stabilized in Muktananda's consciousness. The fluidity with which Muktananda moves from one intuition to another suggests two things: the uneven course of all spiritual development and the full range of teachings embedded in the narrative. Throughout the text there are indications that all five of these intuitions are alive and deepening in Muktananda, but some experiences confirm one and some another. The process does not seem to resemble climbing a ladder. Even after the culminating experiences have irreversibly established the fifth intuition, "I am That," images of approaching and being nourished by some Person of the sacred realm, Goddess or guru, are left quite intact. There is strikingly little sense of "prior" or "lower" intuitions being discarded as others gain in strength. They remain valid and appropriate expressions of the complex truth.

In the Blue Pearl narrative Muktananda is writing both as the devotee of his guru, Bhagavan Nityananda, and as the guru of many of those whom he can reach through his autobiography. It is therefore both a hymn of gratitude to his guru for the transformation in his life and a teaching tale directed toward his devotees and readers.

The folk etymology of the word *guru* traces it to two syllables of the Sanskrit language: *gu*, meaning "darkness," and *ru*, meaning "light." The guru is the one who takes one from darkness into light. Thus Muktananda's account is the story of his guru's grace and power, which initiated the process of transformation within him. However, it is also addressed to anyone struggling with doubt about the very existence of the light, doubt about the possibility of ever seeing it or being seen by it or of eventually realizing a deep inner identity with it. To seekers with such doubts and some desire to learn about their inner nature, this narrative is a guru's teaching.

Elaborations of the Blue Pearl Vision

We return now to a longer section of narrative. We may be able to assess whether it affirms the usefulness and accuracy of these speculations concerning images of the sacred, the yogic *sādhanā*, and the shifting relation of the seeker to the light. We may also note if there are significant elements of the narrative that require further exploration.

> Every day I meditated on the Blue Pearl and had many visions. While I was having this joyful meditation on Neeleshwari, I started to hear music in my inner ear. I heard it first in my left ear. In some book or other it says that, if the *nada*, the divine music, is heard first in the left ear, then one is about to die. Several friends warned me solemnly about this, but I replied that death comes at its own particular time, appointed by destiny, and I kept on with my meditation. I meditated on the Blue Pearl with great love. Besides this music, I began to hear a very fine and subtle sound, still in my left ear. Now I was watching the lights and listening to the sounds, and my meditation became even more intense. I heard the fine, mellow sound of the strings of the *veena*. [P. 138]
>
> It is, of course, true that the dawning of the Blue Pearl brings great peace. If a seeker does not get to see the Blue Pearl, his condition will be like that of an ignorant man who does not see the soul, but only the body. A traveler on the path of realization experiences the Self as a living reality. Sri Tukaram, that blessed jewel among saints who attained full realization of God, says in one of his immortal verses:
>
> *tiḷa evaḍheṁ bāndhūni ghara*
> *āṁta rāhe viśvaṁbhara*
> *tiḷā ituke biṅdule*
> *teṇeṁ tribhuvana koṅdātale*
> *hariharāchyā mūrti*
> *biṅdulyāṁta yetī jātī*
> *tukā mhaṇe he biṅdule*
> *teṇeṁ tribhuvana koṅdātale*

Tukaram Maharaj says in this verse that God, the Nourisher of the universe, lives in a house as tiny as a sesame seed. He is called the Nourisher because He sustains the whole universe. The Lord of the universe, the supreme Self of all living beings, the power of *prana,* who is known inwardly through the higher intuition by yogis, devotees, and *jnanis,* who is the treasure-house of omniscience, has made His dwelling place a house as small as a sesame seed. Just as a huge spreading tree grows from a tiny seed, the Nourisher of all, who manifests Himself in an infinity of forms, shapes, and sizes, has a tiny seed for a house. The tiny seed is the source of the huge tree, the tree is contained in the seed, but the seed has a separate existence as a seed. One seed can grow into a tree, and the tree gives birth to countless seeds that are essentially the same as the first; in the same way, the *bindu,* the divine seed, can manifest in endless ways and forms and yet preserve its original identity. The Lord who lives in the *bindu* never loses His integrity nor His original power. His greatness and glory remain complete and unchanging.

This can be made clearer by another analogy. We know that man is born of a man and that he has all the characteristics of his progenitor. A son is born from one drop of his father's semen, but the father does not lose anything of himself when the son is born; he stays the same as before in all respects, and the son born from his father's semen is as complete as his father. His physical characteristics are like his father's, and so also is his way of behaving. We can say that the father is reborn as his son and that the son is therefore not a son, but the father. In the same manner, God, the source of the universe, creates the infinite universe within His own being by activating the Chitshakti in His own Self. He pervades it and yet transcends it. In other words, He builds His house within His own being and lives in it. Tukaram Maharaj's lines: *tiḷā evaḍhe bāndhūni ghara ānta rāhe viśvambhara*—"The Nourisher of the universe lives in a house as tiny as a sesame seed," are perfectly true, and there can be no doubt or argument about them.

The *bindu,* which is as small as a sesame seed, is the house of the Self. God is inside it—God who is the perfect form of the Self. If you have a vision of the *bindu*, then you should understand that within it lies your Self. It is this *bindu* I have called Neeleshwari, the Blue Goddess, the Blue Pearl. This Pearl is as big as a sesame seed and like a house, and the supreme Self, God, lives in that house. Tukaram says that this *bindu* in fact contains the three worlds within it. Just think—heaven, the human world, and hell are all inside it.

The individual soul is enclosed within four bodies, one within the other, which I have called the red, the white, the black, and the blue. The red corresponds to the gross body, the white to the subtle body, the black to the causal body, and the blue to the supracausal body. The supracausal body is within the Blue Pearl. Through meditation you can fully realize how the three worlds can be contained within a *bindu* as small as a sesame seed. Furthermore, Tukaram says, "The trinity of Brahma, Vishnu, and Shiva come and go within the *bindu*." This *bindu* is the dwelling place of these three gods. Siddha students, now you can understand for yourselves how great, how significant, how sublime is the tiny *bindu* that you see in meditation. God, the supporter of the three worlds, lives within you in the tiny Blue Pearl. Therefore, O man, seek Him within you in reverence for God and in the company of great beings. Until you have searched within, what can you possibly see? You may have seen Paris, London, and New York, but you have only seen a fraction of just this one world. Yet the Lord dwells within you with His three worlds. These things are not meant just to be talked about or heard, they are meant to be attained, and through steadfast practice they will be attained.

The Blue Pearl is a great and holy pilgrimage center. Jnaneshwar Maharaj says:

> *doḷāṅchī pāhā doḷāṁ śūnyāchā śevaṭa*
> *nīḷa biṅdū nīṭa lakhalakhīta*
>
> The eye of the eye, the *neelabindu*, even beyond the void, is brilliant and sparkling.

This radiant and scintillating and sublime Blue Pearl can be seen directly in meditation. O Siddha students, you can have *darshan* of it! But you have to remember that, if you want to see such a great and wonderful thing, your way of life and your habits must be the purest and the most holy. You have to become worthy of it. Your associations, your words, and your thoughts should be full of God. He who has seen the Blue Pearl is the most blessed of all human beings. It is written in the *Skanda Purana*:

> *kulaṁ pavitraṁ jananī krutārthā vasundharā puṇyavatī cha tena apārasaṁvitsukhāsagare' smīnllīnaṁ pare brahmaṇi yasya chetaḥ*
>
> The whole family of a sadhaka in whom Chiti is flourishing becomes holy, because the Shakti makes everything holy. The mother of such a boy or girl herself becomes fulfilled. The earth upon which he walks becomes holy. [Pp. 139–142]

When a sadhaka of Siddha Yoga becomes such a great lover of God, he can sanctify the three worlds. When the supremely ecstatic Chiti begins Her work and when one has the vision of the Blue Pearl, this love arises from within. It is this love that overwhelms the tongue and melts the mind. A student can then purify all his four bodies through meditation. He makes every place where he meditates a holy place. [P. 143]

. . . I am describing the greatness of the Siddha student because his worth increases after he begins to see the Blue Pearl in meditation. In this connection let me give the meaning of one of Jnaneshwar's verses. Remember it. Jnaneshwar says, "I shall dwell at the feet of him who sees the Being who lives between the eyebrows. I shall always meditate on the nature of him who secretly sees the divine Blue Light, which lives between the eyebrows. O people! He who sees the Blue in the space between the eyebrows, he alone is blessed, he alone is fortunate." [P. 146]

There is another verse by Jnaneshwar that I very much like to give—it is like a deity which I worship. It is a great mantra not only for me, but for all those on the path to liberation. Furthermore, what I am going to quote is a testimony of my own inner experience, it is the criterion of realization and the key to the mystery of the Guru. This is why I regard this verse as a mantra. O my dear Siddha students, listen! Read it carefully, as it contains the mystery of mysteries:

> *doḷānchi pāhā doḷāṁ śūnyāchā śevaṭa*
> *nīḷa bindū nīṭa lakhalakhīta*
> *visāvoṁ āleṁ pātaleṁ chaitanya tetheṁ*
> *pāhe pā nirūteṁ anubhaveṁ*
> *pārvatīlāgiṁ ādīnātheṁ dāvileṁ*
> *jnānadevā phāvaleṁ nivrittikripā*
>
> O seekers after the knowledge of perfection, the very eye of your eye, where the void comes to an end, the Blue Pearl, pure, sparkling, radiant, that which opens the center of repose when it arises, is the great place of the conscious Self. Look, my brother, this is the hidden secret of this experience. This is what Parashiva, the primal Lord, told Parvati. Jnanadeva says, "I saw this through the grace of my Sadguru Nivrittinath."

Such is the significance of the *neela bindu*, which I have called Neeleshwari, the Blue Goddess. Just from seeing this Blue Pearl you can attain *jivanmukti*, the state of liberation. But this is not full realization, nor the state of perfection, nor the final goal of the Siddha Path. When you see the Blue Pearl all the time, this means that you are in the *turiya* state, the state of complete transcendence. If a seeker dies after having this vision, he will go to Brahmaloka, the world of Brahman, and attain complete fulfillment by finishing his *sadhana* there.

Now I often saw a wonderfully luminous ball of light. It was much brighter than the other lights, and as I gazed at it, my meditation became better and better. As before, the four lights would appear first of all, and when the Blue Pearl appeared, my mind would converge on it for long periods of time, experiencing extremely joyful repose. My breathing became steady and shallow. When I breathed out, the breath would go only the distance of about two fingers from my nostrils, and when I breathed in, it would go down only as far as my throat, never to my heart. However, I did not pay much attention to this for fear that my meditation would be disturbed; I always took great care that my meditation should remain firm. During this stage, many divine fragrances came to me. They were so fine that compared with them even the finest scents brought to me by my dear devotees were dull and flat. There is no fragrance in the world to equal these divine fragrances, and they made me quite drunk. I floated in ecstasy—they were so divine. The experience stayed with me for a long time. With the coming of these fragrances, my breathing became very short and slow, and a special kind of *pranayama* took place spontaneously. When my breathing was like this, there arose in me the most sweet and beautiful love. It felt like a direct, true revelation of God. Love is God. That is why Narada says in the *Bhakti Sutras* (51): *anirvachanīyaṁ premasvarūpam*—"Love is indescribable in its very nature."

With these experiences of the subtle levels, my enjoyment of meditation increased and increased. My mind was in such an extraordinary state that in every meditation I felt great joy and rapture, and every day this rapture increased so that the bliss of the day before seemed as nothing. I discovered that there is no limit to this kind of joy. Love grows steadily deeper, and there is no final point to love.

With this experience I came to understand that there was still something ahead. Sometimes in meditation everything would abruptly change. My eyes would slowly roll up and become centered on the upper space of the *sahasrara*. Instead of seeing two images separately, my eyes saw one. This is what is called *bindu bheda*. Ah! What a great gift of Siddha Yoga! How mighty the power of Kundalini! What is understood intellectually through books and study can be experienced directly through Siddha Yoga. [Pp. 146–147]

The more I meditated, the longer the Blue Pearl would stand steadily before me, and the longer it stayed, the more its brightness increased. As long as it was there, it would display ever new ways and miracles. Infinite feelings began to well up within me, such as: Is it just blue or is it Neelakantha, Shiva with a blue throat? Is it just blue or is it a blue Sri Nityananda? Is it just blue or is it Neeleshwari, the Blue Goddess, Bhavani Uma Shakti Kundalini? The Blue Pearl came closer and closer. The more it grew, the more it shone, and the more Muktananda grew, the more he changed, the more he opened, the more he expanded and realized what Muktananda really was. Whatever was happening to the Blue Pearl was happening to Muktananda. My faith in the Blue Pearl became still stronger, and just as you think in relation to different parts of the body—"they are mine" and "that is me"—so I came to think of the Blue Pearl. [P. 167]

The Validity of Meditative Visions

This segment of the narrative does more than expand upon the prior experiences with the Blue Pearl. It begins to answer an unstated question, a question shared, I would presume, by anyone who is having or even reading about such visions. "In what sense is this true or real?" One may wonder if what is happening is merely the private, perhaps delusional eruption of the inner world of fantasy. Muktananda himself wondered about these visions, and his efforts to resolve his questions took two major forms. He went often to see his guru, Bhagavan Nityananda, to be reassured that he was still moving in the right direction, and he turned, as the previous excerpt indicates, to the authority of scripture.

In a talk given in 1979, nine years after the Blue Pearl narrative was written, Muktananda addressed the question of how to differentiate between experience that is delusional and that which is both "true" and "real." He had just finished retelling the story of how he came to see the red, white, and black lights in meditation, when he added:

I was perceiving these things. Just by perceiving something, it is not enough; you have to have some proof. The Indian scriptures mention three things, and only if you have those three things can you say that that is true. Something

> can be true only if it is told by the Guru, only if it's written in the scriptures, only if you have had the experience of that. If these three things do not come together, then even if there is something which is true for you, or whether it's true or not true, it's not real. You have to have these three things to make something true. It should be told or shown by the Guru, it should be written in the scriptures, and you should have had your own experience of that.[9]

He then began to quote or to sing some of the verses of Tukaram Maharaj and Jnaneshwar Maharaj included in the long excerpt above. Later in the talk, he described the Blue Pearl and again emphasized that any assessment of a vision's validity needed to consider more than the nature of the private experience and more, even, than the word of the guru:

> Two things came together: what the Guru said and my very experience. I still needed the proof of the scriptures. Even if the Indians say something or the Westerners say something about something, about spiritual matters, if it's not written in the scriptures, then no matter what you say, even if it's true, it is not true if you cannot find any proof in the scriptures. Then I found one of the *abhanga*s of Tukaram Maharaj . . . . Tukaram Maharaj had attained the truth.[10]

The confirmation and reassurance Muktananda felt when he found scriptural support for his direct experience help to explain the teacher's task he has undertaken in the narrative. He is writing in the capacity of the guru or teacher who can validate the parallel experiences of seekers, assuring them not only on his own authority but on the authority of scriptures of this millennium that such visions are authentic, auspicious, and a supreme blessing.

The Attainment of Liberation

The necessity of working within this threefold criterion of authenticity is made all the more urgent by the next segment of the narrative. Here Muktananda turns to the experiences that represent the climax of the yogic *sādhanā*, the attainment of *jīvanmukti* or liberation from the cycle of birth and death. In the yogic scheme of things, this is the fruit of all the purification, the rigorous austerities, and the cumulative spiritual attainments. What follows is Muktananda's unique version of direct, personal experience that, on the one hand, is obtained by obeying his guru's command to go off and meditate and, on the other, is consonant with the traditional scriptural formulation of the state of a liberated being or *jīvanmukta*.

> I was now seeing the miracles of Chiti within the Blue Pearl as well as listening to the *nada*. I meditated every day; indeed, I could not find enjoyment in anything other than meditation. Once in meditation my eyes rolled upward, became inverted, and stayed in that position. I saw a firmament filled with white lights and heard divine sounds all around. My mind became concentrated on this, and I saw an extremely beautiful, shining blue star. It was not the Blue Pearl, but it was marvelously brilliant. It looked just like the familiar planet Venus, which we can see shining in the west in the evening, and in the east at daybreak. This beautiful star is located in the center of the upper space of the *sahasrara*, and it never moves. I watched it for the whole of my meditation. When I came out of *tandra*, I got up and began to walk about outside. I went up onto the hill behind the Gavdevi temple, wondering what the star could have been. I was sitting on the part of the hill where there now stands the Turiya Mandir of Shree Gurudev Ashram. It was all forest then, and I sometimes used to sit alone up there till 8:00 or 9:00 at night. That night, as I was sitting there, a star descended from the sky and disappeared. It was just like the star I had seen in meditation. I was puzzled by this and did not understand it at all. I started to meditate again, and felt waves of rapture and delight and love flow within me. I went on meditating, and the firmament appeared again with the star shining steadily. [P. 139]
>
> Again the blue star shone steadily before me, not moving at all. While I gazed within at the upper regions of the *sahasrara*, I traveled to many worlds with the blue star as my vehicle. It was not the Blue Light or the Blue Pearl, but a blue

star. Though it looked small, it was large enough to contain me. One day it took me far away, and set me down in the most beautiful world, the most entrancing of all those I had seen. I cannot describe its beauty, for words would be an insult to it. In this world I came upon a fascinating path, and, following it, I saw many woods, caves both large and small, flowing streams of pure water, white, blue, and green deer, and also some white peacocks. The atmosphere was very calm and peaceful, and there was a beautiful blue light everywhere, such as you would see if you looked at the early morning sun through a piece of blue glass. There was no sun or moon, only light spreading everywhere. When I arrived I felt such strong waves and impulses of Shakti that I knew intuitively that I was going to have the *darshan* of the ancient seers. I started to move around with the speed of thought. And then what? This was Siddhaloka, the world of the Siddhas! I saw many Siddhas, all of them deeply absorbed in meditation. Each one was in a different *mudra*. None of them looked at me. Some had long, matted hair, some were clean-shaven, and some had pierced ears. Some were sitting under trees, some were sitting on stones, and some were inside caves. I also saw the great seers I had read about in the *Puranas*. I saw Sai Baba of Shirdi. Though Nityananda Baba was in Ganeshpuri, he was here, too. Each Siddha had his own hut or cave or house made in styles I had never seen. Some of the Siddhas were just sitting quietly.

The climate was very good and the light very pleasing. I found that I now knew everything. I recognized the seers and sages of ancient times and, moving on a little, saw many yoginis, all sitting steadily in their various divine *mudras*. I spent a long time wandering around Siddhaloka looking at the yoginis and Siddha saints. I was very fascinated by Siddhaloka. No other world had seemed so good to me. I did not feel like leaving and thought it would be very nice if I could stay. Then I saw a huge lotus pond with golden lotuses growing in it. Turning away from this pond, I saw the Seven Sages in a group, a sight which brought me peace and love; it seemed that someone unknown was guiding me. I entered another forest—very beautiful. I did not recognize the species of any trees in it. I saw more Siddhas there and felt the desire, as I had earlier, to sit down in the lotus posture and meditate. As soon as I sat, the blue star appeared, and for some reason I felt compelled to go and sit in it. I don't know how I did this or who was controlling me. Anyway, the star at once took me back at immense speed to the place where I was meditating.

When I arrived, the blue star passed within me into my *sahasrara* and exploded. Its fragments spread throughout the vast spaces of the *sahasrara*. There was no star in front of me now, but just an ambrosial white light. Then I passed into Tandraloka, which was quite near to me. At that moment a Siddha, whom I did not know, appeared to me from Siddhaloka and said, "You have just seen Siddhaloka, the world of the Siddhas. Here live the great saints who have achieved *jivanmukti*, liberation. There is no hunger, no sleep, and no awakening. One eats joy, drinks joy, lives in joy, and continually experiences joy. Everything there is joy. Just as a fish sleeps in water, lives in water, eats in water, and plays in water, so the inhabitants of Siddhaloka abide in joy. Without the grace of a Siddha, no one can go there. Those who are doing the *sadhana* of the Siddha Path, who belong to the Siddha tradition, and who will attain full Siddhahood will go to Siddhaloka. The blue star, which became your vehicle and took you there, is the only way of traveling to it. It can also take you to other worlds. But until the star explodes, the cycle of birth and rebirth is not broken, the bondage to *karma* is not cut, the veil of sins and good deeds is not torn away. Only when that is torn is the eye of differentiation removed." After he said this and blessed me, the saint disappeared. [Pp. 149–151]

Once while I was in Tandraloka, the secret of my vision of Siddhaloka was revealed to me. Siddhaloka is perfectly real and exists for anyone who attains perfection, whatever his religion . . . . The blue star in which I had traveled is found in the *sahasrara* of every creature. Its brilliance can vary, but its size is the same. And it is also by means of this star that the individual soul passes from one body to another in the cycle of birth and rebirth. However many times a man is burned or buried, the blue star will always stay the same. It leaves the body at death, but stays at the place of death

> eleven days. Afterward, according to destiny, it carries the soul with its sins and virtues to different worlds. The blue star is the self-propelled vehicle of the individual soul. When the individual is born again, the blue star is born with it. When the star exploded, my cycle of coming and going ended. The vehicle had broken down, so how could I come and go any more? This breaking may also be called the piercing of the knot of the heart. In Tandraloka I learned that all the *karma* of my previous births had been cancelled out, and as I learned this, the whole world immediately changed for me. All these experiences were not under my control but under the control of the inner Shakti, because the Shakti is completely independent. [Pp. 152–154]

The attainment of *jīvanmukti*, the summit of the purely yogic *sādhanā*, is not treated by Muktananda as the final step in spiritual evolution. I will return, at the end of this chapter, to his discussion of a major pitfall that awaits one who stops at this level of *jīvanmukti*. Liberation, it turns out, can be not only an attainment but a subtle trap as well.

Explorations in Nonordinary Powers

At this point, however, I would like to continue exploring the yogic path by suggesting that, in one way or another, we may all be able to draw meaningful parallels between the events of the Blue Pearl narrative and our personal experience. What do we know, whatever our cultural tradition or commitment to any formal mode of spiritual seeking, about the processes of purification and power? Can we add to our comprehension of the experiences described in the narrative by reconsidering those moments in our lives that are resonant with Muktananda's evolving *sādhanā*? For me, the most striking parallels connect my experience with several of Muktananda's specific references to the attainment of certain yogic powers.

In an earlier section of the Blue Pearl narrative, Muktananda describes having "visions which were absolutely authentic." In a later chapter of *Play of Consciousness* the same phenomenon is reported in greater detail:

> Next, I saw a light that was different from the red, white, black, and Blue lights, and as it came into view, I saw many, many worlds within it. It was a soft saffron color, and in the middle of it were thousands of soft blue sparks and a soft golden radiance. It was very sweet and lovely. It arose within the series of four lights that I had already experienced. I saw many clairvoyant visions in this new light, so I watched it with great attention. Just as I had habitually passed into Tandraloka in meditation, so I now entered the place within the radiant light. I shall call it Sarvajnaloka, the world of omniscience. The great Indian seers and sages who attained this place through the yoga of meditation became omniscient, and if they wanted to, they could go there even in the waking state. Through the grace of Parashakti, a sadhaka will occasionally reach this state in meditation. When my mind became stabilized in Sarvajnaloka, I could see far away into many different worlds. Everything I saw there was perfectly genuine. Sometimes I would see some accident in the outside world—a factory catching fire or a river in flood—and these things always actually happened. However, it was only through the grace of the Goddess Chiti that I could visit Sarvajnaloka in meditation and see all these things. I could not see them whenever I wanted. I saw many marvelous scenes in meditation. [P. 137]

This passage reminds me of a series of events in my life that began when I read an article by two physicists, Puthoff and Targ, in a book called *Psychic Exploration,* which led me to *Mind-Reach,* a book by the same authors.[11] These men were managing, it seemed, to function as regular scientists and still explore the peculiar world of precognition and what they called remote viewing. They described the ability of such people as Ingo Swann and an amazing police chief named Pat Price to "see" events and places as remote as the inside of a sealed, underground piece of apparatus, the other side of the continent or the globe, or even the other side of two planets soon to be visited by Mariner probes. They could not only describe the way they imagined a place to be but could visualize it as it actually was. For one, the vantage point could be that of an Israeli pilot as he dove into battle. Another might seem to hover in midair over a remote island or some top-secret defense installation, thousands of miles away. They could then draw a map of these places to scale.

During the school term in which I was reading this, I was also teaching a seminar called "Consciousness." When the students responded to the idea of remote viewing with the predictable range of reactions, I said, "Why don't we see if we can do this ourselves?" So we did; we successfully replicated the results that Puthoff and Targ had obtained, using the same elaborate procedures as closely as possible, with a few improvements in design and statistical analysis suggested in the literature since their work. Even if the overall results had been statistically insignificant, my personal experience as subject would have convinced me that the phenomenon of remote viewing was real and important. However, the results for all the trials did satisfy the traditional criteria of replication, which makes it all the more legitimate to explore in detail my own efforts as "remote viewer."

The overall design was straightforward. One or two subjects, either seminar students or myself, would meet two other key figures, called the outbound experimenter and the Mason Hall experimenter, at the loading dock of one of the University buildings, Mason Hall. We all took turns playing the different roles. The Mason Hall experimenter gave the outbound experimenter a large envelope containing ten small envelopes, each of which contained instructions on how to get to a specific location (a golf course, a chapel, or a construction site, for example). The participants had neither helped choose or describe any of the targets nor knew anything about the larger pool from which the day's set was drawn except that each location was within fifteen minutes of Mason Hall.

The Mason Hall experimenter then walked with the subjects to the basement laboratory. Each subject was seated in a simple room equipped with a pad of paper, pens, and a tape recorder. Meanwhile, the outbound experimenter left the area, used a small pocket calculator to obtain a randomly generated number from 1 to 10, counted out that number of envelopes, opened the last one, and went to the target designated on the card inside. Equipped with a camera, paper and pens, and a small tape recorder, the outbound experimenter was then expected to arrive at the target within fifteen minutes and spend fifteen minutes at the site.

The subjects, meanwhile, sat in their rooms in the basement laboratory. The Mason Hall experimenter knocked on the door of each room to signal the start of the fifteen-minute period during which the outbound experimenter was presumably at the target. The subjects were instructed to try in any way they saw fit to imagine and then record their impressions of the location and activity of the outbound experimenter. They could draw pictures, dictate into the recording machine, or write notes. They were allowed a few minutes at the end of the fifteen-minute period to finish recording their impressions, verbal or otherwise.

Meanwhile, the outbound experimenter dictated a narrative of the route taken, sights seen, time of arrival, and any other observational details. In addition, he or she took at least four pictures at the target site and then, at the end of the fifteen-minute period, returned to Mason Hall. Once all of the data had been properly filed away, all of the participants went to the target location to look around.

The data were transcribed and organized into ten separate subject folders and ten separate outbound experimenter or target folders. Ten judges were recruited from several psychology classes. They were volunteers with some interest in the phenomenon of remote viewing but no knowledge of the design of this study. In turn, each of the judges was given one subject folder, containing the subject's drawings, notes, and/or transcribed dictation, and all ten target folders, each containing the pictures taken and the transcribed narrative of the experimenter for a single day. Each judge was asked to compare the one subject folder with all ten target folders and rank their correspondence. Rank one would be given to the folder the judge deemed to be the most likely to have been the actual target for the day when the subject produced the data in his or her subject folder. Rank ten would be assigned to the folder that seemed the least likely to have been the actual target for that day. The average rank that a group of randomly guessing judges would be expected to arrive at is 5.5, and the statistical question in this study was whether the actual average of the ten judges was significantly closer to rank one than the chance expectation. In fact, it was. The statistical test revealed that only once in a thousand times would one obtain such a deviation from the average rank expected from randomly guessing judges. Something was "going on."

I had never been a subject in any tests of extrasensory perception. I had guessed my way through the Zener deck of various patterns a few times, but had never shown any talent for it. My sense was that some people were good at it, but not me.

During my first trial as a subject in our study I sat in my small lab room, without knowing what to do or expect, very dubious about my capacity to visualize anything, least of all the target site, when suddenly a clear picture of the University Hospital appeared in my mind. I was standing on the ground, and the building seemed to stretch endlessly above me. I remembered who was playing the role of outbound experimenter for that day, and thought, "Oh, Duke must be at the U Hospital." But then I remembered that Targ and Puthoff had warned against making specific guesses, so I tried to clear the image from my mind. Suddenly another scene appeared: I was looking up at an overpass from the foot of a hill near the train station. I thought, "Maybe that's where he is, at the train station." But when I tried to draw a picture of this and the previous image, I found myself drawing mostly a series of arrows, pointing upward. Beside them I wrote the words, "Up. Attention directed upward." I reported some other imagery consisting of curves and arches, but there was nothing else I wanted to record about the target.

Where had the outbound experimenter actually gone? In fact, he had never left the building complex. His assignment had been to go first to one elevator in the complex and then to the other and ride up and down for the entire fifteen minutes. When I accompanied him to the target site after the data had been placed in an envelope, I felt both delighted and crushed. I had been preoccupied with "upness," and that was certainly part of his experience, but I felt certain that no judge would match my data with the actual target location since I had produced images of the hospital and the train station. I was right; the judge didn't see the correspondence that I had seen and rated the actual target as only the fifth most likely to have been the target on the day I generated my data.

If that had been the sum total of my experience as a subject, I would have continued to be impressed with other people's extrasensory capacity but not my own. However, the studies continued.

I had even less self-confidence when I began my second trial as a subject. It occurred to me to sit very quietly at first and try to clear my mind. As I did so, there followed a series of visual images so sharp and intense that even now, four years later, I could easily show a movie cameraman where and how to reproduce the entire sequence. In fact, the images had the quality of a vivid dream or movie, particularly in their fluid, shifting perspectives. I had the distinct sensation of riding over the Fuller Street bridge, and I knew somehow I was seeing what the outbound experimenter, Sharon, was seeing out the window of her car. I was seeing a brilliant green playing field and at the same time feeling, viscerally, a sustained right turn along but away from the field itself. I saw white football goalposts, a broad field, and then numerous barriers made of chain link fencing and an elevated tennis court. Suddenly, my perspective shifted, and I saw the trees across the road that flanked the old abandoned municipal course where I had played golf many times, twenty years before. Again, my perspective shifted, and I was on a low hill, farther along on the course, looking out over an expanse of yellow flowers. As I was dictating my impressions, I recorded my firm sense that Sharon was north of town, and asked out loud, "What's the name of that road, parallel to Plymouth, along the river?" The name I couldn't remember was Fuller Road.

The actual target that day was the Fuller Road pool, a new complex built on the site of the old golf course. When Sharon returned to the loading dock, I rode back with her to explore the target. We drove over the bridge and swung right along the playing field with its intensely green grass. There were the goal posts, though they were for soccer rather than for football. The scale of the scene wasn't quite the same as my image of it, but it was fairly close. We arrived at a standard chain link fence inside of which stood the pool, which, for Sharon, had been the main focus of the target. Since no one had been using the pool when she arrived, she had sat looking at the sun dance on the choppy water and had tried to do whatever one does when one "sends" an image to someone a mile away. Had the sun's yellow reflection in the pool registered as the yellow flowers I had seen? This was the only fit between subject image and actual target that seemed open to dispute. The rest was very obvious, to us and to the judge who ranked the Fuller Road pool folder first out of all the targets he compared with my subject folder. And, for more personal bemusement, there was my clear impression of being on a golf course when in fact the target hadn't been so used for more than a decade.

I participated in one other trial as a subject; my performance was similar in that I seemed to know something about the direction in which the outbound experimenter was headed. I dictated a very specific description of the route I sensed she was taking, and it corresponded exactly to where she had driven. The rest of the imagery, however, wasn't accurate at all. Nevertheless, in ranking my folder correctly, the judge wasn't distracted by the inaccurate imagery because the directional description was so specific and valid.

The next trial that I will describe, the strangest of all, took place during the winter, and we all knew that the outbound experimenter would be on foot. This time I was the Mason Hall experimenter rather than a subject. I was feeling bored, waiting for the time to pass before I would knock on the doors of the lab rooms and terminate the run. I was struck by an impulse to put some "good vibrations" into the atmosphere by meditating. I thought that if the subjects picked up some peaceful vibrations, the images that came to them might be more accurate. As I began to meditate, a scene flashed in front of me. It had the smoothness and uncanny fluidity of a scene being photographed by a slowly moving camera. I was able to watch the changing scene from the vantage point of that imaginary camera. What I saw was a moving point of focus gliding along State Street, past the old Ad Building to the Student Union. Then it was as if the camera stopped and sighted along the long sidewalk that led to the International Center in the Union. I was absorbed in the scene when the focus shifted abruptly to a glistening hardwood floor and ten red and white bowling pins. The scene was so framed that I could see nothing but the bowling pins and a little of the alley.

Two thoughts raced across my mind in rapid succession. The first was, "Maybe the target for today is the bowling alley." I knew that there was an alley in the Student Union, but I had never been there; nor did I know exactly where it was. The second thought was, "I'm going to ruin the experiment. What if the subjects start picking up on my images rather than the actual target?" So I tried to erase the images from my mind and concentrate on the clock and my duties as the experimenter. Time dragged again, so I decided to relax and meditate for a while. Within seconds, I was seeing the same truncated view of a bowling alley, except that this time I saw the machine rising up, the bar sweeping the fallen pins away and then lowering the three leftmost pins to the alley. I tried even more vigorously to remove the image from my mind, and soon it was time to knock on the subjects' doors.

I listened carefully as the subjects related what they had seen, but to my relief they had seen neither the bowling alley nor the Union. When the outbound experimenter returned, we all retraced his route along State Street, up the stairs and into the main entrance of the Union, and down to the bowling alley. I couldn't contain myself. I asked what he had been doing while he was there, but neither he nor anyone else had been bowling. He had thought that the subjects would receive the image best if he played the pinball machine, so he did that and left. It was dark on the side of the room where the bowling alley stood. I was feeling uneasy. We started to leave and were nearly at the top of the stairs when the outbound experimenter told me to look back. A woman had started to bowl. We watched as she knocked down seven pins. The machine came down, cleared the area, and set up the three leftmost pins for the woman's second shot. I ran up the rest of the stairs. It was eerie enough to have seen any bowling pins at all, but to have seen, half an hour before, the same pattern of three pins being lowered by the machine was overwhelming.

Conjectures on Remote Viewing

The experience of seeing, vividly and unmistakably, the target location chosen for that day had a very peculiar effect on me. Beneath my amazement and delight, behind my fantasies of moving from one successful experiment to another, I found lurking a real aversion to the exploration of remote viewing. In part it came from some disturbing sense of the uncanny, the weirdness of having succeeded at the task. In part it came from my conviction that the great teachers of many cultures and eras must have had good reason to caution, as they did in no uncertain terms, against becoming absorbed in such petty, ordinary tricks as these. Most concretely, it seemed a ridiculous misuse of meditation, and I was glad to turn my scholarly interests in other directions. Still, the memory of those experiences constantly prods me: What conclusions can I draw from them?

The best that I can do is list, in a rather unsystematic fashion, some of my thoughts or the pieces of some incomplete, complex answer that have occurred to me over the years:

1. Remote viewing experiences or, as Muktananda terms them, "visions which [are] absolutely authentic" are real and provide important data for human beings, especially psychologists, to study and understand.

2. They seem to be associated with an atypical, nonordinary, or meditative state of consciousness that has something in common with both the unforced, spontaneous state of dreaming and the sudden rush of insight "arriving full-blown in the brain," to use Pearce's description.[12] It simply doesn't have the same feeling and sequential unfoldment as thinking, guessing, or hypothesizing.

3. I feel completely on the wrong track whenever I start imagining that these events involve a sender (the outbound experimenter), a receiver (the subject), and a physical message superimposed on some sort of carrier wave. It all becomes a hopeless tangle of false analogies to radios and television sets.

The puzzle revolves around a complex set of questions: When there were several thousand people within a fifteen-minute drive of Mason Hall, why did the location of one person, the outbound experimenter in the Fuller Road run, for example, come so clearly to dominate my interior visualizations? And how could events that had yet to happen in ordinary clock-time, as in the bowling alley run, have affected my visualizations in the lab, or was that simply an amazing coincidence? In telepathic or clairvoyant phenomena, there is a relatively fixed array of percepts (those the outbound experimenter experienced and recorded at the target site) and a vast pool of internal imagery (the subject's experience) which is not totally free but certainly wide open, unstable, and, evidently, capable of both converging on the actual target site and stabilizing there. My apparently precognitive image of the bowling machine leaving the three leftmost pins was replicated in reality, half an hour later. If telepathy and precognition reflect a single underlying process, what lawful relations between the consciousness of one person and that of another, or between one person and the physical universe, are implied by these phenomena?

I have no grand, final answer to my own questions, but I do have a hunch that emerged from the remote viewing experiment about how reality "works." There seems to be a process shaping the flow of events, be they mental or physical, gently nudging them as far as they can be nudged toward providing us with a glimpse of a remarkable truth. Our mental life, to take that example, contains a most dazzling array of thoughts, images, memories, and sensations. They swirl around, mostly far from the level of conscious awareness. Imagine then that we are sitting in the remote viewing lab, half trying to visualize the location of the outbound experimenter and half wondering how to stop trying so hard. There we are, and all the while that vast reservoir of imagery is swirling around inside us. Something works to shape that inner world by strengthening the closest approximations to the actual target. Why? Simply because they are the closest to the truth of the matter. The actual target or some aspect of it—its "upness," its color, its direction from town, the visceral sensation caused by turning right to reach it—becomes the basis, as it were, of some inner adjustment of the strength of the most accurate approximations in our mind. It reminds me of the game where the one who knows the secret location guides the one guessing by saying, "You're getting cold . . . colder . . . warmer . . . very hot."

We are nudged toward realizing the truth of the matter until a spontaneous visualization explodes into our conscious awareness. We see or just "know about" the target or some significant aspect of it. But why? What is the purpose of the nudging? My answer is that we are nudged if we are ready to have and learn from an experience that reveals our deep interconnectedness with other apparently separate beings. Our imagery and thoughts are shaped until they reach the startling, but still manageable, perception of some event that is indeed remote. If we don't want it to happen, it tends not to. If we aren't ready to handle the version of reality contained in that experience, it tends not to happen. But, conversely, if a vision of Oneness, and our part in it, is already laid down in our awareness at some level, and if it is already bearable, then remote viewing is one way that reality works to confirm the validity of our intuition.

My hunch boils down to an assertion that the nonordinary powers we manifest, inside or outside of the laboratory, are the workings of the universe as teacher. We can have experiences that are catalysts for a process of personal transformation. One realization along the path of power and purification is that gaining personal power and yielding to a larger or higher power are not contradictory developments. The accurate remote viewing image seems not to be something achieved but something received. It comes to us "unbidden." It can be blocked, and hence the active pursuit of purity of body and mind, but it cannot be forced.

I began the remote viewing experiment with two questions, "Does this really happen?" and "If so, why?" I ended up convinced by my own experience that it happens. I am still wondering why, but I am also wondering, "If it doesn't happen, why not?" Our power to register the location of the outbound experimenter seems to be lessened or blocked altogether if we have nothing swirling around in our imagery that can be amplified by the process that, in effect, whispers to us, "Yes, that's it." One way to restrict the range of our imagery is to "guess" where the outbound experimenter might have gone. Guessing not only serves to narrow, prematurely, the range of available imagery. It also stirs up fantasies of being "right" and receiving recognition for one's talents. These fantasies soon disrupt the natural flow of images that are possibly related to the actual target. Many of the reasons why remote viewing fails to happen can be traced to the operation of what I explore, in a later chapter, as the ego. What is being purified is the ego, and what emerges as this process proceeds is power, often a power we call nonordinary.

Some might take exception to the notion of a universe governed by a sportive God or Goddess who juggles the odds to further some cosmic hide-and-seek game being played with us mortals. They might prefer to see remote viewing, precognition, and/or telekinesis as examples of the impersonal tendency toward order or symmetry that is at least part of the supreme principle underlying the universe. I would not argue with such a view. In fact, it doesn't seem to be especially different from my own. I simply prefer a somewhat more lively and personalized version of what is operating behind or within remote viewing. As with any mnemonic device, my version is useful only to the extent that it keeps reminding me of an order of reality that I tend to overlook, forget, or deny.

Does this long sidetrack into the realm of remote viewing add anything to our understanding of the Blue Pearl narrative? In searching for the implications of Muktananda's experiences I find it useful to explore their consequences. How he was changed, by both his remote viewing experiences and by his visions of the Blue Pearl, is a powerful clue as to their meaning and purpose. It is clear that all the lights, sounds, *kriyās*, and instances of remote viewing moved Muktananda toward a profound transformation in his own understanding of the true nature of things. The question, "What was behind all these experiences?" is really the same as asking, "Who was behind the process of transformation?" Muktananda's answer is, "The Goddess." This assertion is not an invitation to debate the truth of theistic constructions of reality. It is an assertion of the power and extensiveness of the source of the transformative process, which needs a name but certainly exists even without it. The name Muktananda uses is the Goddess, Chiti Kundalinī, and the main point of the first section of his narrative, in my view, is that it portrays the systematic infusion into one aspect after another of Muktananda's inner and outer life of the transformative process that he attributes to Her.

The Blue Pearl narrative and my experiences with remote viewing have had the effect of reducing my tendency to deny the validity of reports, such as, "This happened" by conceding only, "Well, he thought that it happened." The psychologist often follows up this undercutting of the reported occurrence by a further distancing, "The question is, 'Why did he *think* that was happening?'" In contrast, the seeker who simply accepts the report asks the more personal questions, "What does this person's experience tell me about reality? What can I learn from it? Can I find, in my life, moments of similar import and understand them more fully than before?" I have come to appreciate all those who study yogic or nonordinary powers because they expand the common image of our human potential. Even if each expansion is followed by a contraction, a doubt that it did occur or ever could occur, the trend is toward a far grander conception of the power of the human mind than psychology had contained before such studies were undertaken.

The Process of Purification

Returning to the issue of purification, we see illustrated many of the same principles illustrated by the phenomenon of remote viewing. As we have found in our exploration of yogic or psychic powers, ordinary consciousness is unnecessarily blocked. Involuntary movements of one's physical body, emotions, or utterances are called *kriyās*, and the yogic understanding of what is taking place is that a powerful energy is encountering a blockage, a constriction, an impurity. What sorts of experience have any of us had that would help us understand these expressions of the process of purification?

The range of mental and physical experiences that fall in this category is enormous. Few Westerners are familiar with the ecstatic behavior that earned the Quakers their appellation, or the Holy Rollers theirs. Few have seen or experienced the movement of the Spirit in charismatic renewal movements or in rural churches. What all these forms share with each other and with the yogic path we are exploring is a tendency to discern the sacred in the spontaneous, the involuntary, and the uncontrollable. From this perspective, our ordinary state is understood to be excessively preoccupied with being in control of everything. The image is of a battle, a struggle to let go, to allow the unforced, the state of grace to predominate over the limited, self-protective ego.

Muktananda often likens the inner workings of the purification process to the ascension of a serpentine power through a series of blockages from the base of the spine to the top of the head, where this ascending, female power, or Shakti, is reunited with the eternal, changeless power, Shiva. All of this is understood to occur in a structure that is homologous to the physical body, usually called the subtle body. The clash of power with obstacle that takes place during the process spills over into the physical body as a *kriyā*. Muktananda tells of his eyeballs rolling around so violently that his friends were worried about him, and he attributes these *kriyās* to the piercing of subtle blockages, or *chakras*, in the region of the eyes. In other passages he tells of roaring like a lion at night and frightening the local villagers.

I have experienced these involuntary movements of the body—head arching back, breath accelerating or stopping, feelings of intense pressure in parts of my skull—as startlingly new events, and yet they were fully anchored in my prior experience. They were anchored in such deeply ingrained distinctions as natural versus forced and free versus controlled. We have all had scores of experiences that prompt such phrases as "Suddenly, something in me . . . ," "Some inner reservoir of energy . . . ," or "I don't know how I managed that because I couldn't do it again in a hundred years." These may be split-second dramas or uncanny, undeliberated responses to sudden demands, but from them I suspect that we come to know our "natural self," or whatever we might call it, and be in awe of its potential. *Kriyas* are unique in that the arena in which they occur is virtually self-enclosed and private. The struggle is internal. If the onset of these spontaneous movements is sufficiently gradual, one can usually block them, but often one chooses not to. Why?

A *kriyā* is an expression of an inner understanding. It is a very complex understanding, but to some extent it can be articulated: There is some Other, some force, manifesting in or as my body or my mind. It is all right for that to happen. It is really the same power that I have known all my life, sometimes most dramatically in times of crisis. I know it as my own truest Self, which is functioning to protect me, to assist me, to control me. Now it is working not to rescue me from some emergency or external situation but to effect an inner transformation, removing whatever blocks prevent me from experiencing it more fully in my life. I could resist it, but why should I? I will yield to it, either until its effects have run their course or until my own fear, doubt, and pain have set counteractive maneuvers in motion. The evidence of this internal struggle may be virtually anything—violent contortions of the body, slow and occasionally painful movements into strange postures, yelling, making noises. What matters is the intention of the power, and that intention is healing and benevolent. The wisdom of the power lies in its selection of involuntary acts that match the unique obstacles of my mind and body. The power is intelligence itself, and my goal is to become a less obstructed vehicle for that intelligence.

How one courts the process of purification is at least as interesting a question as why one would do such a thing. The Blue Pearl narrative describes one way in which it can be done: One meditates with great enthusiasm and discipline, endures much austerity, and then considers whatever happens to be the blessing one has sought. The only purpose of the purificatory process is to enable one to advance in one's development. In Muktananda's case one fruit of this process was the vision of the four lights, culminating with the vision of the Blue Pearl itself.

Whereas *kriyās* are a sign of inner battle and purification, visions and the graceful, spontaneous meditative experiences of tastes, the odor of perfumes, and the sound of celestial music are a sign of the free-flowing, divine inner energy. What are we to make of the content of such experiences?

The Vision as Manifest Content

We have become so accustomed to the traditional descriptions of heaven, celestial chariots, or thrones, that we often have only two possible responses to such reports: acceptance or rejection. The first accepts the content and modifies any previous imagery accordingly. The second dwells on the discrepancies among various spiritual accounts, decides that there is no useful factual information here, and dismisses the whole idea of heaven or a sacred realm. Thus, we work our way through millennia of scriptural accounts and other recorded visions equipped with nothing but the most self-limiting of questions: "How can I believe that?" And by "that" we mean, of course, the manifest content of the report—the seraphim and cherubim and all the rest.

What we reveal in all this is our tendency to confuse the verbal form of an idea with the idea itself. We can grasp, and repeat, the words that describe an experience, but we tend to forget that the words are but a meager representation of the original experience. At the end of centuries of such confusion, we arrive at the modern university, where clearly the verbal form of an idea is so predominant that other forms, symbolic visions, for example, do not seem to be ideas at all. But that is precisely what they are.

Visions are the manifest content of a latent, intuitive idea about reality. They are a bringing to the surface of some deeper understanding. Sometimes they so powerfully and effectively make manifest a latent understanding that the experiencer finds them an infinitely better mode of representing that understanding than the verbal mode could ever be. Often the vision is accompanied by the conviction, "I could not possibly be creating this experience myself. This is a gift. This is a blessing." The visual content, the attribution of causality, the verbal account, the later explanations, and the emotions stirred by the experience are each important expressions of the same fundamental, latent understanding. When our response to a visionary account is, "Well, that's beautiful, but what does it imply?" we may be insisting that only when the vision is encoded verbally will we grant that anything of importance has happened.

Just as the manifest content of a dream may be traced to a profound truth held but not yet acknowledged by the dreamer, so too a vision may express the experiencer's as yet unacknowledged and perhaps inexpressible sense of the truth. What Wilber calls the deep structure of a person's consciousness is most important here, and thus the manifest content should be examined as symbol and not treated as something merely to be accepted or rejected, believed or not believed.[13] I am not trying to discount verbal formulations, mathematical equations, or any other mode of bringing one's deep structure into the best possible conscious approximation. I am only asserting that many kinds of self-representations have been appropriate for different people at different times. The Blue Pearl vision is certainly the product of one of those intensely vibrant, creative moments. Muktananda's growing understanding found a satisfactory mirroring in the evolving imagery of the Blue Pearl.

A Pitfall on the Yogic Path

The yogic *sādhanā* that this chapter describes reaches the traditionally defined goal of liberation, *jīvanmukti*. However, at this point in his writing Muktananda steps back from narrating his experiences to emphasize both a potential pitfall and the incompleteness of the experience of liberation. Several passages from *Play of Consciousness* attest to Muktananda's sense that he had not completed his spiritual journey simply by becoming a *jīvanmukta*. One such excerpt follows:

> My meditation became more and more subtle. At this stage, meditating yogis have to be extremely careful. Through the vision of the Blue Pearl they will certainly achieve liberation, but they will not be able to attain complete realization of Godhead; their experiences will only be partial. For full realization one has to enter within the Blue Pearl to the inner Self. [P. 139]

In the 1979 talk quoted earlier, Muktananda is explicit about the danger of a premature sense of completeness, and he shows how crucial his guru's intervention was at this point of peril. In this account he narrates how he felt after experiencing the momentous visions that signified his attainment of *jīvanmukti*:

> So I began to revel in that blue dot. The more I watched it, the more I loved it, the happier I became. I thought, "That was it!" At this point I was very proud and I went to meet my Baba [Bhagavan Nityananda]. Baba said, "You have a long way to come. Go, just go. Right now, leave this place." I thought that I had attained everything. He said, "You're still far away." I turned back and went back.[14]

Back he went to his meditation hut at Suki, and what happened next is the subject of the chapter that follows. In wrongly concluding that he had reached the end of his spiritual journey, he had fallen into the trap of pride. Muktananda's narrative starts out with tantalizingly pleasurable yogic experiences and seems to conclude with the attainment of liberation, but, in fact, it does not conclude without an admonition and a larger teaching. The admonition, which he passes on from his guru, is to block the pride of attainment and set one's goals farther than yogic experience, even beyond the experience of liberation. The teaching is that the yogic path is only one of many paths, all of which are necessary. Muktananda is suggesting a larger synthesis of many paths, a form that we have not yet discussed.

The Synthesis of Spiritual Paths

How do the various modes of seeking fit together? How are the paths of purification, devotion, and understanding reconciled into one coherent approach to the sacred and the goal of all spiritual development? History records many violent struggles between the followers of different paths. According to Pagels, the early Christian church suppressed those teachings that fostered the seeker's intuition of his own divinity, the Christ within, in favor of a more dualistic, devotional teaching that emphasized the Otherness and historical uniqueness of Jesus Christ.[15] Fox explores the tensions between the Celtic and north European shamanistic trends, which emphasize attunement to nature and the body, and Roman Christianity with its emphasis on a transcendent God that tends to bring to the fore issues of separateness and sinfulness in the flesh.[16] But are these three paths always antithetical?

The Blue Pearl narrative suggests that they are not. Muktananda conveys the traditional teaching of a synthesis in Indian spirituality that has evolved slowly over the past four or five thousand years. There are, to be sure, yogic themes in his autobiographical narrative—a concern for accumulating power, endurance, and purity of body and thought—but they are not divorced from themes of devotion and understanding. In contrast to Patanjali's *yoga,* Muktananda continues a synthesizing tradition, sometimes called *tantra,* with deep roots in the history of Indian spirituality. It joins together the heroic, will-centered yogic approach with the devotional theme, as focused primarily on a newly emergent central figure: the Goddess. The tantric modification of *yoga* preserves the experiential, experimental approach of *yoga* but casts the seeker's existence and progress into a clearer relationship with the Other, the Goddess Kundalinī or Chit Shakti mentioned throughout the Blue Pearl narrative. In the process, the devotional theme, emphasizing the necessity of the guru's guidance and grace along the path, merges with the familiar yogic themes of purification and effort.[17]

Swami Muktananda draws heavily not only on yogic and devotional texts but also on the teachings of the Upanishads and a lesser known system of thought, the Trika school of Kashmir Shaivism. This tantric school incorporates and balances all of the three themes that we have been discussing. Dating from the ninth century A.D., the Kashmir Shaivite tradition associated with Vasugupta and developed by his followers over the next four centuries combines (1) the liberation-in-this-lifetime, energetic style of *yoga* and early *tantra* with (2) the devotional relationship between Parvati, the Goddess, and her consort, Shiva, or between the devotee and the Goddess, or between the disciple and the guru, and (3) the nondualistic teachings concerning the Supreme Consciousness, Paramashiva, the one Self, the one underlying conscious energy of the universe. The purpose of the spiritual quest is to realize, to make real, that inner Self, that one reality.

Muktananda refers to this synthesis as Siddha Yoga. This term connotes pursuit of all the paths outlined above: the yogic path of practice before and after the teacher's initiation or awakening of the seeker's latent spiritual energy; the path of devotion, love and obedience in relation to the Other, whether it be the Lord, the Goddess, or the fully realized guru; and the path of unity awareness, as experienced and taught by the enlightened beings whose lives are the primary teaching of their nondualistic understanding. In the Indian tradition, a teacher who can initiate a seeker, function as guru, and communicate the full realization of all three component paths is called a Siddha guru.

The synthesis of the three paths of purification, devotion, and understanding which Muktananda calls Siddha Yoga is evident even in the segment of the narrative treated in this chapter. Although the yogic processes of purification and power dominate the imagery of the narrative thus far, there are numerous devotional references to the Other, as Goddess and as guru. The path of understanding, as well, is beginning to emerge; over the course of his experiences, Muktananda is coming to view the Blue Pearl as "mine," and even as "me." However, the tone and import of the next two segments of the narrative are in striking contrast to this first, more yogic phase of Muktananda's journey.

3 ▪

IMAGES OF DEVOTION

The path of devotion brings to the fore the seeker's sense of relationship with the Other. How real, how present, how benign is the Other? Muktananda's threefold criterion of a true experience—that it be firsthand and not merely hearsay, that it be told or shown by the guru, and that it be supported by scriptural authority—has special bearing at this point. Muktananda was only gradually made aware of the scriptural precedents of the direct, yogic experiences reviewed in the last chapter. In contrast, the visions presented in this chapter are consonant with the Indian devotional tradition that had affected him deeply from his earliest youth.

The Direct Encounter of the Other

The Indian scriptures are filled with examples of devotees having the *darshan* of the Other. What Muktananda was lacking was his own direct experience of that *darshan*. As he put it in a later interview with an American scientist, "In India, the people believe in the reality of the personal form of the Lord. There was a time when I did not accept it. The different manifestations are given names such as Rama or Krishna or Durga. But after I had the vision of the Blue Pearl, and after I saw all the manifestations appearing within it, I accepted their reality. That is the secret of the yoga of meditation."[1] Muktananda is frank about his position at the time of the events that occur next in the Blue Pearl narrative. He had been sent back to his meditation hut after being told in no uncertain terms by his guru that his spiritual journey was far from over. And he did not, on the basis of his direct experience, accept fully the reality of the personal form of the Lord—not, that is, until the events that continued and extended his vision of the Blue Pearl. It is to these events and "the secret of the yoga of meditation" that we now turn:

> O my dear Siddha students. Now something new happened. Listen to this with love, and don't ever forget what I am telling you. One day I was sitting in joyful meditation. As soon as I sat down, I started the great worship of Sadguru Nityananda, who is one with the Goddess Kundalini Shakti. "O Gurudev, you are on my east, you are on my west, you are to my north, you are to my south. O Sadguru, you are above me, you are below me. O Dear Sri Guru, you are in my eyes, you are in my ears, you are in my nose, you are in my mouth. O Sadgurunath, giver of grace! You are in my throat, you are in my arms, you are in my chest, you are in my back, you are in my stomach. O mother Guru! O father Guru! You are in my thighs, you are in my legs, you are in my feet. O my Baba! You are in me, I am in you. And you are in any difference there may be between my form and yours." I invoked my Guru in this way, and my meditation began with the red aura glittering before me. Then the white flame, the black light, and the Blue Pearl followed one after the other. My heart was filled with joy. Megharaja, lord of the clouds and friend of yogis, was thundering inside the *sahasrara*. Then a great miracle happened. I should not talk about it, but Sri Guru is urging me to do so. I do not have the strength to write about this miracle. My hand does not move. My fingers have stopped working. My eyes will not open. Only my tongue is moving. Perhaps Nityananda has come and forcibly taken possession of it. Since I do not have the right to speak, it is Bhagavan Nityananda who is speaking. My friend Yande is doing the writing. He has surrendered himself to Baba Nityananda, which is why he is writing.

The wonderfully radiant Blue Pearl, with its countless different rays shining from within, came closer to me and began to grow. It assumed the shape of an egg and continued to grow into human shape. I could see it growing with my own eyes and was lost in utmost amazement. The egg grew and grew until it had assumed the shape of a man. Suddenly divine radiance burst forth from it. For a moment I lost consciousness. What had happened to Tandraloka? Where had Sarvajnaloka gone? And what had become of the intuitive intelligence by which I had understood everything so far? Muktananda forgot himself for a few moments. Because he did not exist, everything else also disappeared. If there is no one to see, there is nothing seen. If there is no one to listen, there is no sound. If there is no one to smell, there is no smell. For a moment I was not conscious of anything. However, my state of meditation was still just as it had been. I was sitting firmly in the lotus posture, facing north. Then, I again saw a shining human form in place of the oval. As it shone, Muktananda came back to himself. Muktananda's Tandraloka returned. Intuitive intelligence came back and also Muktananda's extraordinary memory, which was always watching over and reporting his inner states.

The egg-shaped Blue Pearl stood before me in the form of a man. Its brightness lessened. I saw within it a Blue Person. What a beautiful form He had! His blueness shone and scintillated. His body was not the product of human fluids derived from the seven elements, but of the blue rays of pure Consciousness, which Tukaram Maharaj called *chinmay anjan*—"the lotion of Consciousness that grants divine vision." His body was composed of infinite rays of Consciousness. He was a mass of Consciousness, the essence of Muktananda's inner life, the real form of Nityananda. He was the true form of my Mother, the playful, divine Kundalini. He stood before me, shimmering and resplendent in His divinity.

What a beautiful body He had! What beautiful eyes! What a fine straight nose! What attractive ears and earrings, and what beautiful hair! How fine His head! He had no beard. He wore on His head a crown set with the nine jewels. These were not inert material creations of this earth, but were composed of pure Consciousness. What beautiful long hands, slender fingers and nails He had—all so blue. The clothes He wore were soft and fine. How long and shapely His legs, and how well formed His toes. His whole body was exquisitely beautiful. I kept gazing at Him, from head to toe, from toe to head, my eyes wide with amazement.

He came toward me, making a soft humming sound, and made some kind of gesture. "Say something," He said. What could I say? I was completely absorbed in just looking at Him. He walked right around me and stood still. Then, looking at me, He made a sign with His eyes. Then He said, "I see with this foot, too. I can see everywhere. I have tongues everywhere. I speak not just with My tongue, but also with My hand, and with My foot. I have ears everywhere. I can hear with every part of My body." Thus He spoke, and I listened to Him. "I move with My feet, and also with My head. I can move any way I like. I move as far as I want in an instant. I walk without feet and catch without hands. I speak without a tongue, and I see without eyes. While I am far, far away, I am very near. I become the body in all bodies, and yet I am different from the body." Then He said a little more, which was heard by Nityananda and cannot be written here. Then he added, "This very way is the path of the Siddhas, the true way." He lifted His hand, and made a gesture of blessing. I was utterly amazed. As I watched, the blue egg, which had grown to a height of six feet, now began to shrink. It became smaller and smaller until it was once more Neeleshwari. It became my Blue Light, the Blue Pearl.

I was completely amazed. Filled with great bliss and thinking only of the grace of Sri Gurudev Bhagavan Nityananda and of the divine Sri Chiti Kundalini, I passed into Tandraloka. I realized that this was the *neela purusha,* the Blue Person, who grants the realization of God with Form. He is also called the supreme unmanifest Being, by whose blessing one proceeds to the realization of the ultimate Truth. After blessing me, this Being returned into the Blue Pearl from which He had emerged; and then my meditation ceased.

How marvelous are the countless visions in the world of meditation! How great is man's worthiness! How magnificent is the Blue Pearl! How bountiful is Dhyaneshwara, the lord of meditation! How glorious is man, how magnificent he is! O Muktananda! You are great. You are infinite. You are extraordinary. I was completely overcome with joy, giving thanks for my human birth and recalling what I had seen. Now the conviction "I am the Self," became firmly established. I believed completely in *So'ham hamsah,* "He is I, I am He"—"You are God, God is you." I began to experience the full realization of this truth.

I was convinced that this was the divine Being who had been described in the [*Bhagavad*] *Gita* (13:13–14):

> *sarvataḥ pāṇipādam tat sarvato kshiśiromukham*
> *sarvataḥ ṣrutimalloke sarvāmavratya tiṣṭhati*
>
> He has hands and feet everywhere. He has eyes, heads and faces on all sides. He has ears everywhere. He knows all and exists pervading all.

> *sarvendriyagunābhāsaṁ sarvendriyavivarjitam*
> *asaktaṁ sarvabhruchchaiva nirguṇaṁ guṇabhokti cha*
>
> He has all the qualities of the senses and yet is without any of the qualities of the senses, unattached and yet supporting all, free from the three attributes of manifestation and yet enjoying them.

He dwells in the *sahasrara* and appears in subtle form in the powers of all the sense organs. He can be experienced by the senses and yet is far beyond them and without them. While in the body, He says, "I am Muktananda, I am, I am," yet He is unattached to it. He is the nourisher of all. He is the sustainer of every cell within the 72,000 *nadis,* the One who nourishes by giving vitality to the vital fluids and richness to the blood. He is beyond the three *gunas,* and yet, even though He has none of the *gunas,* He dwells within the *sahasrara* and experiences all *gunas.* If someone gives food, He eats it; if someone gives flowers, He accepts them; if someone gives clothes, He wears them; if someone bows, He accepts that too. The person giving all these things thinks, "I am giving them to Baba," but it is He who accepts them:

> *bahirantashcha bhūtānāmacharaṁ charameva cha*
> *sūkshmatvāttadavijneyaṁ dūrasthaṁ chāntike cha tat*
> ([*Bhagavad*] *Gita* 13:15)
>
> That is without and within all beings, the unmoving and also the moving, unknowable because of its subtlety, and near and far away.

He pervades the outer and inner aspects of the movable and immovable creation—men and demons, birds and animals, insects and germs—but because He does so in His subtle form, He is not understood. People think that He lives far away, but He lives very close to you, in the middle of the *sahasrara*. This supreme Being appears to be different in different people, races, actions, names, forms, countries, and times, but He is undifferentiated. He lives as human being in a human being, as bird in a bird, as cow in a cow, as horse in a horse, as man in a man, and as woman in a woman. What else can I say? He becomes all things and is yet unique. He gives His strength to all created things. Like a mother He protects and sustains them and then gathers them all into Himself. He is the supreme light of all lights; all lights take their brightness from Him. There is no darkness about Him. He knows everything about everything. If this were not so, how could Muktananda have recognized the Blue Person? What I had seen was the Blue Pearl; it was Shiva, the Blue Lord; it was blue Nityananda, who is the highest object of knowledge, who is the gift of Kundalini's grace received in the highest states of meditation, who is apprehended only with the knowledge acquired in Sarvajnaloka, and who dwells in His total fullness in the heart and in the *sahasrara*. O seekers! He is within your Blue Pearl, but do not think that you have become perfect just because you have seen the Blue Pearl. That supreme unmanifest Being is extremely secret to *sadhakas*; He is the goal of the Siddha Path. This is not something that can ever be expressed in speech or writing, even at the end of time. It is only by His grace that divine realization will come. Siddha students will understand how this matter, which should not be written, has been written. I am compelled to speak, and dear Yande is taking it down.

But even with all this, my contentment was still incomplete. There was still something left. The stage my meditation had reached was very divine. The Blue Person I had seen is also known as the Sphere of unmanifest Light. Yogis see Him, who contains the entire world within Himself, within the Blue Pearl in meditation. I was now meditating on Him and constantly remembering Him. He had settled in the land of my mind and had taken a form. I meditated constantly and always saw the sweet, radiant Blue Pearl in its infinite variations. Its luster was more dazzling at each moment, and my enjoyment was forever growing. I was meditating in the *sahasrara* and was also hearing the divine *nada* of thunder. As I listened to this thundering, my meditation became so joyful that the desires which remained in my mind were smashed by the thunder and just disappeared. As I listened to this sound for a while I experienced complete union with the taintless Parabrahman. [Pp. 168–173]

After my vision of the Blue Person, my meditation became stabilized in the upper space of the *sahasrara,* where I saw a celestial radiance like a mist, and in the midst of this radiance, the Blue Pearl. This brightness increased day by day. It is always found around the Blue Pearl, and it is said that the radiance of the firmament within the *sahasrara* comes from the splendor of the Blue Pearl. I meditated on it every day, and each day there arose the awareness, "I am the Self." Sometimes I would also see the Blue Pearl moving in and out of the *sahasrara* for short periods. If you ever have a vision of the coming of a great saint, you should understand that it is all happening through the agency of the Blue Pearl. [P. 174]

I had best preface any comments about the path of devotion and this fragment of the author's experience of *bhakti* by joining Muktananda in admitting that words will not get us very far. There is at least some comfort in knowing that in this realm we will not be prone, as the Zen teachers caution, to confuse the finger pointing at the moon with the moon at which we are pointing. These are unspeakable moments. Perhaps, however, this very fact can turn us to a useful starting point. Muktananda writes, "I should not talk about it . . . . My hand does not move." Why not? What is holding him back?

As he recalls the visionary events, he is once again overcome by the same awe, rapture, and surrender that he felt some fifteen years earlier. His inspiration to record these events, which he knows are not usually revealed by saints or spoken of only "in veiled language in their poetry,"[2] is sustained by turning the physical task of writing over to Yande, a close devotee of his, and attributing the more crucial act of narration to his guru, Nityananda, who is speaking through him. Such is the intensity and the form of the devotional relationship to the Other that emerges from this section of the narrative.

The State of Meditation

Muktananda's meditative experience of the *darshan* of the Other brings us to the question, "What is meditation?" How shall we think about a process that leads to events as enduring and transformative as those recorded in the Blue Pearl narrative?

Some meditative experiences come from the deliberate practice of tuning out the world of sense impressions and somehow allowing the mind's chatter to subside or to become peripheral. As a result, one's awareness is dominated more and more by representations of deeper, more fundamental layers of one's understanding or one's being. However, the formal practice of meditation should not be confused with the goal of the practice, the state of meditation, which may be entered via many other routes. Saul, later known as Paul of Tarsus, was the only one on the road to Damascus who comprehended Jesus' words and saw the blinding light. This was a meditative *darshan* experience. Its reality is not diminished by the fact that his companions did not hear or see the same thing. On the other hand, some visions, such as that of the Virgin Mary at Fatima, are shared by many people in a collective, meditative moment of *darshan*. What, then, is the defining characteristic of meditation?

There are many possible answers to this question, but one of them is structural. We can consider each moment's experience as a structuring of numerous disparate elements, some of which are sense-bound, some of which are memory-bound, and others of which are the amorphous, not even necessarily verbal intuitions of our many-layered consciousness. From all these elements we form gestalts, patterns of meaning and willful, expressive action. If we ask of any moment, "What is the central organizing element that dominates the current gestalt?" we may find that sometimes it is external and sense-bound; sometimes it is a complex of memories and emotions; sometimes it is an idea that sets up meaningful categories in our mind. Sometimes, however, the best or only word for what is manifesting through the structure of our awareness is the Self.

According to Patanjali's account, as meditation deepens, the structure of our consciousness becomes increasingly focused, until in one final movement even the last, single point of focus is gone. *Ekāgratā* is his term for intense concentration on one point.[3] Thus, driving at high speed, threading a needle, and paying rapt attention to a movie all share something in common with the process of meditation. However, in its fullest sense, the meditative moment represents a structuring of consciousness that is centered on the Self. The more that consciousness is centered on the Self, the deeper is one's meditation. To put it in other but equivalent terms, centering on God is meditative or contemplative prayer. Images of the Self or images of God can become the content of the meditative encounter: The light, the voice, the Blue Pearl, the Blue Person, the silence, the All. Thus, the last point of focus, in Patanjali's analysis, reveals the sacred as the Center, while the ensuing *samādhi* or enstasis reveals the sacred as the seamless Whole, but both are valid and powerful images of the Self.

The contrast drawn here is between a structure of thoughts, images, and experiences centered around the Self and one that slides off-center and organizes around some lesser point of reference. In true meditation, all perceptions, thoughts, or memories stand in relation to the Self. They are open to the sacred by being connected to the Center, located in a boundaryless Whole, and seen as composed of and reducible to their Essence. As our consciousness moves back toward its ordinary and everyday form, the Center is obscured by the apparent, but in fact illusory, importance of desire-related or emotion-charged elements; before long, the familiar cycles of pain, excitement, and boredom have replaced the meditative state.

Similarly, as the apparent but illusory need to build fences, make invidious comparisons, and protect that which is near and dear come to dominate our consciousness, the meditative sense of an unbounded Wholeness yields to the fearful world of division and enmity. Finally, as the common denominator, the Essence of all the diverse elements of awareness, is overshadowed by the seeming incomparability of one thing or quality to another, we return to the chaos of a disordered multiplicity.

Muktananda's account of seeing the Blue Person in meditation adds to our appreciation of the sacred in that it shows how the primary image of the Self can be the beloved Other, the one that blesses, teaches, and transforms from its place in the devotee's heart. This expands the possible variants of meditative consciousness to include any awareness, including the waking state, that is open rather than closed to the possibility of *darshan*. The sacred as Person is a potential reference point for considering the cause, the meaning, and the resolution of any event. To function with an awareness of that sacred referent is to be in meditation. The devotional path stresses constant remembrance, a constant opening to the divine Person in a spirit of reverence and gratitude.

It may seem that an either/or has been created: *either* we are in a meditative state that centers around some image of the Self *or* we are attentive to "outer things." The traditional injunctions to "have done with the things of this world" or to turn away from "sense pleasures" suggest that we do have to choose, and it is better to choose the "inner" as the access route to the sacred. This advice, however, is merely a reflection of how powerful is our tendency to allow outer events, and our ordinary perspective on them, to block our access to the sacred. It is not an assertion that there exists a forced choice between the two perspectives, inner and outer. It is possible, and in fact is the goal of meditation, to surmount the apparent either/or and remain fully attuned to the sacred, to the Self, while fully awake and alert to the details of the everyday world. Our attitude toward the outer world is at issue here. It is our tendency to allow desire, fear, and other such dynamisms to block meditation that is being called into question, not "the world" or the fact that we live in it. The question is how we live in it, and the path of devotion shows us the possibility of a continuous sense of *darshan*, a continuous sense of relationship with the sacred Other throughout all aspects of our lives.[4]

Explorations in Devotion

Muktananda's meditations and his subsequent narration of their content place a difficult demand on us. As we read, the text becomes the focus of our outward-turned mind. In all probability, it evokes various mental and emotional reactions. How, then, can we avoid sliding into states that tend to block meditative structuring of our consciousness while we attempt to make sense of another person's accounts? My solution to this problem is to allow the text to remind me that I, too, have had moments of *darshan*. I, too, have experienced that awe-filled, magical sense of encountering the sacred. It takes persistence to overcome some inner, carping voice that points out how puny my experiences are compared with the *darshan* of the Blue Person. How could merely walking in the woods and being frozen in my tracks by some cathedral-like array of sun and leaves be considered in the same domain as Muktananda's experience? But why should I dwell on the disparity? What matters is that such experiences formed my own introduction to meditation, although the word was not yet part of my vocabulary. Such experiences serve as the basis of the gestalt which forms around one very important expression of the Self, the sense of the sacred in nature's awesome perfection. It is in that spirit that I explore and share the sequences of *darshan* experiences that began to suggest to me the qualities and full context of devotion.

A brief, two-scene vignette comes to mind. Muktananda had just arrived in Ann Arbor. I was fascinated by him, but also terrified. I went to the ashram during the informal morning periods but sat as far away from him as physically possible. My eyes were riveted on him, but I hoped I was safely out of his range. During *darshan* I would watch people approach Muktananda, bow, offer him some small gift, or ask a question or two. I formed an impression and soon shared it with one of his long-time devotees. "It seems to me," I said, "that Muktananda is pretty remote, pretty indifferent. People don't seem to matter to him very much."

"Oh," came the immediate reply, "He's like a mirror. He reflects your inner state. Maybe you're just seeing your own remoteness." There seemed to be no ill-will in the rejoinder. It even seemed quite plausible. Still, I swallowed hard and attempted to absorb the unexpected confrontation with myself that had developed.

The second scene took place at an Intensive, an overnight retreat, a week later. This time, as I stood watching dozens of people approach Muktananda for *darshan* and heard the rippling laughter that spread around him, I saw him as a fountain of love. He was just sitting there, pouring out warmth and tenderness, lightening each person's heaviness by being totally at ease, totally himself. As I watched this scene the devotee's words came back to my mind: "He's like a mirror." It occurred to me that, by that logic, if I were seeing him as a fountain of love, then I myself must be a fountain of love. For the next few moments I was delightfully suspended between appreciation of the scene I was watching and appreciation of who I must evidently be in order to recognize the moment for what it was.

A more complex, three-scene sequence of my encounters with the path of devotion also comes to mind. The first scene took place at the same autumn retreat. I had made a great effort to meditate, but it was now the fourth hour-long period in two days. I was beginning to wonder whether meditation would ever seem easy and pleasant to me. Between the noisiness of my neighbors in the meditation hall who were experiencing intense physical *kriyās* and the mounting complaints from my back and knees, I was ready to quit trying altogether. The only alternative seemed to be to open my eyes. I did so, feeling somewhat naughty and defiant. There I sat in a small, darkened room full of people meditating, and there, twenty feet from me, was Baba Muktananda sitting in his chair. He seemed so peaceful, so self-contented. As I watched him meditate, he turned his head in my direction, our eyes met, and the space between us filled with two golden ribbons of soothing light. The sensation was not simply visual. These golden beams of light appeared to be moving in a full circuit, out of his right eye into one of mine and out of my other eye and back to him. The flow was palpable, gentle, and pleasurable. As the connection grew stronger, I felt tiny puffs of air against my cheek, and without any visual image to support the thought I concluded that the air currents were being caused by a tiny hummingbird hovering at the level of my eye. My internal voice announced, in a tone of amazement, "My goodness, I'm a feeding station for a saint." I seemed to be a repository of some subtle nectar as well as the recipient of a caress of air from this tiny creature's wings. The moment passed, and I was left somewhat dazed—dazed and very pleased.

The second scene took place nearly a year later. My wife and I had traveled to Arcata, California, for a month-long retreat. Muktananda had been sick and arrived halfway through the month. It was not as easy this time to make contact with him, both because the number of people had multiplied tenfold and because he was under doctor's orders to rest more and talk less. Thus, with some doubt that we would be able to speak with him, we waited one foggy morning to say goodbye before returning to Michigan. He came down the stairs, turned toward his car, and then spun around to greet us. In the excitement of it all I reached out to shake hands. He extended his left hand, and before long we were standing there with all four of our hands awkwardly clasped. What soon overpowered my awareness was the unbelievable softness and gentleness of his hands and his grasp. It was, as in the autumn retreat, a moment of connection that contained at its essence an unexpected and wholly convincing gesture of undemanding affection.

The third scene in this sequence took place in the Ann Arbor ashram the following winter. Muktananda was in Oakland, and my sense of connection with him had weakened. I had begun to wonder if the relationship was going to endure. One morning, after we had finished chanting the *Guru Gita*, the director of the ashram walked over to me. As he did so, I tentatively held out my hand to shake his, but he extended his left hand. Our handshake became an exact replica of that final four-handed farewell in Arcata. This time it seemed to be an unmistakable message from Muktananda that all of my moping around about weakened connections was just nonsense. There was such a strong sense of the earlier scene being replicated that I was cast into a very peculiar state of mind.

I didn't realize just how peculiar it was until after I went home, finished breakfast, and drifted into the living room. I put on a record, Schumann's Piano Concerto in A Minor. The music seemed to grow louder and louder; it was sweeter and had more dimensions to it than any music I had ever heard. Before long I was surrounded by a misty brilliance. My breathing was deep and rapid, and my head seemed to be expanding. Waves of pleasure and vitality washed over me, and the familiar inner commentator pronounced, "Well, that's it. It's not just that I am happy right now. It's not even that I am a happy person. It's that *I am happiness itself*. I am an infinite reservoir of happiness. That's who I really am." These sentences rang with truth, and I sat there savoring them for a long time. Tears of joy accompanied the immense relief I felt upon reaching such an understanding.

One conclusion that I draw from recalling these *darshan* experiences is that they can best be understood in the context of our understanding of meditation. There is no question in my mind that no one except Muktananda would have seen the two ribbons of golden light. This does not mean that I was uniquely privileged, that I was the only one to see what was "really there." It means that my waking but nonetheless meditative state was presenting me with a visual image that mirrored my internal state and revealed a growing sense that I was "connected" to this man in a way that was both startling and enjoyable. It doesn't matter that only I would interpret that second four-handed greeting as a message from Muktananda. The vision and the message are mental phenomena that derive from a numinous substructure centering on the Self. Clearly, what stands out most vividly in these phenomena is the presence and message of the Other. How can we understand this?

Devotion and Self-Awareness

In the moment of *darshan*, in the emergence of the Blue Person from the *bindu*, for example, the Other says, "I exist, I am, and I am with you." The inevitable surge of joy attests to one's condition prior to the experience of *darshan*: the state of separation, of doubt, of merely hoping that what others say is true. The cycle can be repeated again and again; each time the moment of *darshan* succeeds, as no other experience can, in giving us the reassurance that we are not hoping in vain, that there is in fact such beauty, love, purity, contentment, and magnificence in the world. The Other does exist, and even our memories and doubt-ridden hopes fall short of the actuality.

We find that odd, magical thoughts survive our usually critical self-censoring. We sing ecstatic songs of praise. Muktananda's hymn to the glory of the Blue Person is but one of thousands of such outpourings of devotion in his and other cultures. Praise the Lord, "praise Him and magnify Him forever," says the Psalmist.

Not only does the Other exist, not only do I see the Other, but I am permitted to look. And I dare to keep on looking. Or, as in the narrative account, there sits Muktananda in meditation, beholding the Blue Person, "eyes wide with amazement." It is a visual love feast. What does the Other reveal about himself? What he says goes even beyond the idealization of the one gazing at him. He describes the Blue Person's nature as unlimited and totally free, and the measure of this lies in his transcendence of the dualities that still exist in Muktananda's mind. He is far and he is near, the same as and yet completely different from such forms as bodies, existing both in form and as unmanifest formlessness. The Other's otherness is most fully conveyed in the paradox and the *koān* because the categories of ordinary thought will not support these mind-expanding revelations of the sacred. The coup de grace comes when the last trace of dualism, the egoic sense of identity that one thinks is certainly different from the sacred Other, turns out to be but another guise of the supreme Being: "While in the body, He says, 'I am Muktananda, I am, I am,' yet He is unattached to it." The Other is not trapped by its manifestation. It is still supremely free, but it is not radically different from anything or anyone.

Every attribute of the *darshan* experience that emerges from the Blue Pearl narrative is also an attribute of meditation. Meditation makes all objects sacred, vivid, fully alive, and filled with meaning. Because it centers fully on the Self, true meditation leaves nothing untouched by the sense of sacred presence. A gradual decline in the predominance of empirical and logical truths and a corresponding increase in one's access to the Self, expressed through the image of Person, are complementary aspects of meditation. Finally, meditation alters one's mental attitude, the most important change being the shift from perceiving the world to be "either x or y" to asking "Why not both x and y?" In this context we turn to the import of *darshan* for the question, What is the relationship between who I am and the Other?

The two answers found in the Blue Pearl narrative, "We are different" and "We are the same," seem to coexist comfortably, and that in itself is a clue to the nature of meditative *darshan* and the role of devotion in a full spiritual life. Could there be a more convincing account of what it is like to encounter the Other than that of Muktananda, who after fifteen or more years is so overcome by the memory of the miracle of *darshan* that he cannot write it down and does not feel that he has the right to describe it? What does gratitude convey but the sense of being in relation to the Other, the source of grace? Yet these expressions of "We are different" are not treated as if they negated or were negated by the statement "We are the same."

What appears to be a polarity, identity versus difference in relation to the Other, turns out not to be a hardened either/or. The entire sequence of devotional experiences appears to be more like an upward spiral that contains both "poles" and integrates them in one cumulative learning process. In my own experiences of *darshan* and in the narrative about the Blue Person there is a direct connection between *darshan* of the magnificent Other and a significant change in self-appraisal. The text swings easily from glorification of the Other to an awareness of the greatness and the infinite, extraordinary nature of all human beings including Muktananda himself. The meditative state delivers glorious versions of the Other and of one's own nature and then links the two: "I am the Self," *"so'ham,"* or "He is I, I am He."

In my own case the linkage seemed self-evident. The direct correlate of perceiving Muktananda as a loving, serene, content, and magnificent being was a series of intuitions about myself: "Then, I must be a fountain of love, too," "I'm a feeding station for a saint," and "I am happiness itself." The moment of paying rapt attention to the Other flows into the moment of self-love, and the two categories that had seemed eternally separate, me and not-me, begin to merge as each appears in the light of the common integrating category, the Self. They begin to merge, and then they fly apart as some new moment of *darshan* propels one's perception of the Other to higher levels of magnificence, sending the spiral upward to yet higher forms of self-affirmation and merger. The process leads to a conclusion about the sacred that recurs in many cultures: At the core of all being there is a playful, joyful dance, found in moments of apparent difference and moments of return and reunion.

The Moment of Initiation

Muktananda's narrative of his encounter with the Other and with the Self suggests some of the ways in which the path of devotion evolves. We may, however, still wonder how it all begins. What is the origin of Muktananda's *darshan* and the sense of his own glory that follows? Where does Muktananda begin the story?

He begins with his initiation, at the age of thirty-nine. He had already been a swami for almost twenty years and a wandering *sādhu* for even longer. Initiation thus was not his first step on the spiritual path. It did, however, mark an abrupt transition in the tempo of his evolution. It occurred on August 15, 1947. Muktananda's description begins with these words: "What an auspicious day! How full of nectar it was! How divine! What merit and great fortune it brought with it! It was the happiest and most auspicious day of my life, the great day of many births and ages. It was truly holy; yes . . . yes, it was the dawn of the most auspicious of all auspicious days."[5]

The events of that day of initiation, that *divya dīkshā* day, are recounted with a sense of reverence and gratitude that mounts steadily. Muktananda's guru, Bhagavan Nityananda, approached him in the morning and offered him his sandals to wear, to which Muktananda replied that he would never wear them, but he would worship them all his life. Then, Muktananda writes, "He looked into my eyes once more. I watched him very attentively. A ray of light was coming from his pupils and going right inside me. Its touch was searing, red hot, and its brilliance dazzled my eyes like a high-powered bulb. As this ray flowed from Bhagavan Nityananda's eyes into my own, the very hair on my body rose in wonder, awe, ecstasy, and fear."[6]

Nityananda offered him some cooked bananas, some traditional articles of worship, and a blue shawl. He instructed him in both the external practice of repeating the mantra *Om Namah Shivaya* and the internal awareness of "I am Shiva" and "All is Om." As Muktananda left, he entered a state of unity consciousness, a state of awareness of the One in the many. The entire world, inside and out, had become a mass of "tiny, scintillating, blue sparks." And, as Muktananda writes, "Even today I can still remember that experience of oneness. I still see those tiny blue dots."[7]

Within days Muktananda's guru had sent him away, to his hut in Suki, with the command to continue meditating. How did these meditative experiences of the Blue Person arise? They arose from initiation, from what Muktananda later understood to be the ancient form of transmission of grace from a saint to a disciple, the process called *shaktipāt*. What Muktananda refers to as Siddha Yoga begins with and is defined by that transmission of energy, or Shakti, and grace into a seeker.

The mind of one whose life is filling up with internal and external meditative experiences of *darshan*, with the sense of being blessed, naturally follows the trail backward in time, seeking to know how all of this happened and where it began. The trail stops when nothing before it seems to be the cause of that "most auspicious of auspicious days." That moment is time zero. On that day one's new life begins, and it begins with the astounding good fortune of receiving the Other's energy, grace, and love. One is called. One is blessed. What defines the discontinuity inherent in this moment for Muktananda is his conviction that no merit or attainment on his part is in any way the condition for or the cause of this turn of events. But even if nothing one possesses or has become is responsible for the events that unfold, still there is something about the seeker at the moment of initiation that must not be overlooked.

In one sense, initiation suggests a cessation, an ending of all the planning and efforts of one's past. There is an opening, a self-emptying that is a crucial preparatory step. It is a rebirth, but the "little death" that precedes it is part of the beauty of the whole sequence. In letting go, in abandoning all willful self-steering, the seeker is creating the space for the influx of energy and grace.

We can invoke the imagery of the path of devotion, the open heart, the surrendered devotee, and the humble spirit, to answer the fortunate devotee's amazed question, "How can all this have happened?" The answer has a dual focus: the readiness of the seeker to be initiated and the gift of the Other. Muktananda's sense that the Other "has done it all," that "He is doing everything" permeates the Blue Pearl narrative. Devotion allows the maximum asymmetry to exist between the active Other and the passive seeker, the fullness of the source and the receptive emptiness of the devotee. These constructions are fully congruent with the idea that meditation is nothing one "does"; it simply happens. The emptying process that precedes the shining forth of the light of the Self in meditation is the "little death" that precedes initiation. Thus, the entire meditative process begins with and is sustained by a series of openings to the Other. There is a giving of disciple's grace, through openness and readiness, and a corresponding receiving of grace.

The inner *darshan* of the Self follows exactly the course of the external drama between Muktananda and his guru: first, a process of becoming detached from both pleasant and aversive memories, a letting go, and then *shaktipāt*, the dawning of a state that is filled with the light of the Self. The path of devotion has the same form on the inside as on the outside, and what often follows the inner *darshan* is a radically altered answer to the question, "Who am I?" The consummation of devotion and that of meditation are one and the same: the casting aside of limitation and separation, the welling up of gratitude and love, even self-love, and a structure of consciousness in which meaning flows more and more directly from the inner Self.

Obstacles on the Path of Devotion

It might seem that a reasonable extrapolation from these scenes of increasingly intimate *darshan* would be simply more of the same, until some point of union were reached. We might imagine a gentle, rather romantic finale to the evolving relationship between the seeker and the Other. Perhaps such a sequence would fit the narratives of other seekers, but not Muktananda's. In the next chapter we find that the transition beyond "Yes, He exists; Yes, we see each other; and Yes, He is within me" is neither gentle nor altogether pleasant. Whereas the process of *darshan* begins with a letting go and an initiation and is sustained by awe and love and gratitude, ultimately one must confront the final obstacle: fear.

Muktananda's fear was of "being destroyed." The Other, "the Sphere of unmanifest Light" that he was encountering, left no room, seemingly, for anything but itself. One day, in meditation, this sphere "opened up and its light was released." Muktananda was overwhelmed by the brilliance of millions of suns. "The light was so fierce," he writes, "that I could not stand it, and my courage broke down." He could neither move nor resist its pull. He cried out for help, "O Goddess, O Sadgurunath, save me!" His *prana*, his life force, seemed to be leaving his body, and he fell down as one dying, making strange noises and urinating involuntarily. It seemed to Muktananda that this was the moment of his death. Over an hour later he regained his waking consciousness and got up, laughed to himself, and said, "I just died, but now I'm alive again." He felt "very much at peace, very happy, and very full of love" and knew that he now understood death to be nothing but this encounter with the Light. He writes that since then "the place of fear within has been destroyed. I have attained total fearlessness."[8]

The limit had been tested and found not to be psychic obliteration or physical death but liberation from the effects of one's own mistrust and feeling of separation from the Other. One barrier to love, fear of the Other, had been removed. If one can untangle the lifelong tendency to compound a yearning for the Other with a terror of closeness, if the terror is confronted and defeated and the yearning is fulfilled, then one has reached that extraordinary transformation of consciousness which in the Indian tradition is called final realization.

Before we turn to Muktananda's meditative representations of final realization, there are several significant aspects of devotion that we must examine. Muktananda's vision of the Blue Person reflects only one facet of the evolving relationship with the Other: his awe, his love, his sense of being blessed, and his yearning for more of the same. We begin to form an image of the magnificent, tender, beautiful Other. However, there is another side of *sādhanā,* including Muktananda's: the drama that joins together the fiery, demanding, testing Other and the resistant, not yet fully surrendered devotee.

It would be misleading to consider only the loving moments and to ignore the equally important times when the Other seems frustratingly insensitive. The glorious periods of initiation and *darshan* may be followed by more difficult periods when the devotee is ignored, insulted, or sent away by the teacher. These tests are as integral as the blessings to the full relationship between the devotee and the Other.

Some of my own experiences come to mind. I recall arriving at Muktananda's Oakland ashram feeling tired and rushed after a cross-country flight. Lunch had just ended. My wife and I were whisked past the registration desk because Muktananda was giving informal *darshan* to about thirty people clustered around him in the courtyard.

The people sitting on the ground made way for us, and we were ushered to a space in front of his wicker chair. His translator recalled our names and the ashram we attended. Muktananda greeted us very warmly and asked a few questions about our trip. Then we all sat quietly for a moment. Suddenly, he shifted the position of his legs in such a way that his heel hit me in the forehead right between my eyebrows. I was jolted by the hard blow, and a chorus of inner voices began to well up: angry outcries of pain, insinuations about his clumsiness and his lack of consideration. This inner, private rumble grew and grew, until the translator's voice said clearly but softly, "That's guru's grace." The anger vanished abruptly, as if commanded to do so. What replaced it was an entirely different interpretation of what had just taken place. I recalled all the stories I had heard about unlikely and seemingly harsh initiations, and I realized that the blow I had received had been utterly benign. At that point, Muktananda told someone to make sure we were given some lunch, and we left.

The event traced a pattern that would recur many times in the following years. Ambiguous situations would stir up my anger or resentment or sadness, but ultimately I would see that they had been yet another blessing and act of grace. Each frustrating, picayune ashram rule, each abrupt change in the barely familiar order of things, each flash of the teacher's seeming anger or indifference could take me to a fork in the inner road. Down one path would emerge yet another round of my own hair-trigger responses of anger and misunderstanding. Down the other, the first stirrings of these immature reactions would, fortunately, be overtaken by a sense of acceptance. It is much easier to see that the Other is benign when everything seems beautiful and lighter than air, but when one is provoked and the ambiguity mounts, then the learning (the unlearning, really) can begin in earnest.

I could list dozens of times when I watched Muktananda blaze with reproach at one of his staff members—the man making the announcements, the chief cook, the harmonium player. Even those times when I was merely an on-looker were sufficient to bring me to the fork in the road. "Poor guy," I would say to myself, aching with empathy for the victim of Muktananda's tongue-lashing, "He must be so hurt (or bitter or depressed)"—only to find that the victims (or at least the few I knew well enough to question later) had taken the other fork in the road and had experienced no such anger or bitterness or depression. Somehow, they had seen only the truth of Muktananda's reproach and only the love and concern that prompted the dressing down. Naturally, they found my empathy irrelevant and uncomprehending.

The fact of the matter is that an ordinary devotee is filled with far more than yearning and gratitude. There are innumerable ways in which a devotee's response reveals the presence of inner resistance. One simply cannot hide it, although sometimes one tries. Actually, there is no reason to hide it. A devotee may fear that resistance will be met with rejection, but it is difficult to imagine a real teacher who hasn't encountered a great deal of resistance and who isn't fully aware of its positive role in the process of growth. The devotee who is least able to progress in his *sādhanā* is often the one who is pretending that he feels nothing but acceptance and trust. This is why the teacher continues to test him. The devotee needs to know the exact limits of his trust and obedience, not because mistrust and disobedience are wicked, but because his limits mark the perimeter of the real relationship that is developing between teacher and devotee, and no internal "prettying up" of that actuality will serve the devotee's development.

There is widespread recognition among the world's religions that cursing God may involve a far more productive concentration of energy in God's direction than some bland pretense that there is nothing holding one back. I watched many people meet Muktananda for the first time, and what always struck me was that he seemed to be more attentive to, to embrace more fully, those who openly expressed their resistance or fear. When a man in the *darshan* line said defiantly, "I can't bow down to anyone, and I don't believe in God," Muktananda, with great warmth, answered, "That's not very important, really. What matters is being able to bow down to yourself and to believe in yourself." Once it has surfaced, the resistance may turn out to be directed against nonexistent pressures and demands.

I recall a young woman who asked him a question with great trepidation and then burst into tears at his answer. When he asked her what was the matter, she said she thought he was making fun of her. He leaned forward and with an amazing mixture of firmness and tenderness said, "A *sadhu* could never do such a thing as that." The young woman brightened up, as though in discovering that there was someone who could not possibly do such a thing she had experienced both an enormous relief and an unexpected blessing. However, it was necessary for her to express her resistance in order to break through to the *darshan* she eventually could recognize and accept from Muktananda.

There is something in us human beings that will passionately defend what we know to be a barren, insufficient plot of land, even while our better judgment tells us that the larger whole we resist is our only salvation. We block our own expansion, our assimilation into a more ample and balanced system. We seem to provoke the teacher's explosions of apparent anger, as if we know that, on our own, we are incapable of simply letting down the barriers and yielding the small space we call our own.

Perhaps everything we do looks different from the outside than it looks and feels from the inside, but this seems to be especially the case on the path of devotion. If you look on from the outside, you may see either inexplicable expressions of love, acquiescence, and gratitude or equally inexplicable endurance of what seems to be abruptness and abuse. However, ask someone who is on the inside or closer to the center than yourself, and all the meanings change. What the mistrustful outsider considers to be slavish, obligatory devotion is, to the insider, an uncontrollable, almost unintentional flow of the natural love of the universe. What the critical outsider considers to be hyperbole or formulas of unfelt adoration, the insider feels to be pathetically inadequate descriptions of the Other's beauty or glory. What the outsider considers to be masochistic endurance, a reveling in the teacher's abuse, the insider experiences as appreciating a necessary storm that sweeps away the inner obstacles to surrender. The storm takes nothing from the insider that he wanted to keep. It takes away only the blinders and the blockages, and the result, a less encumbered devotion, enriches rather than impoverishes. But how can the outsider know that?

Muktananda's meditative vision of the Blue Person, its awesome and entrancing beauty notwithstanding, was not the final stage of his *sādhanā*. His contentment was "still incomplete." As he did from the climactic events of his purely yogic *sādhanā*, the attainment of liberation, Muktananda turns from the experiences that are a consummation of the path of devotion, the supreme *darshan*, to emphasize that the goal of *sādhanā* is beyond even these experiences; it involves a synthesis of all valid paths. The goal is final realization of the Self. Just as his yogic experiences led him to the pitfall of pride, which he avoided through the humbling *darshan* of the Blue Person, the glory of these devotional experiences led him to another pitfall, that of settling for an incomplete understanding. What still lay before him on his *sādhanā* were the understandings of the path of *jnāna* and the visionary experiences by which he represented these understandings to himself. Only through this further revelation and awareness to which we now turn would he reach the goal of full and final realization.

4 ▪ IMAGES OF UNDERSTANDING

The final section of the Blue Pearl narrative brings us to an outcome that is shocking, difficult, and probably not part of the religious or spiritual literature with which most of us are familiar. We are presented with an image of the end of the journey. The goal is attained; something has become real, irreversibly stable, and every prior state appears, in retrospect, to have been a pilgrim's progress through the world of becoming. All the elements of the meditative journey, intuitions of the sacred, the Other, and the Self, converge into one world view, one profoundly transformed attitude toward reality.

Images of Self-Realization

Muktananda's narrative offers us a rare glimpse of the way in which this final state can be represented within the awareness of the meditator. This concluding section of Muktananda's journey attests to the perfection of the Blue Pearl as an ever changing, expressive, and symbolic form, whose shifting appearance mirrors a shifting understanding at the deepest levels.

> Now the awareness of the Self began to rise within me spontaneously. Formerly the feeling *deho'ham*—"I am the body," had always throbbed within me; but now it had all

changed, and it was the feeling *shivo'ham*—"I am Shiva," that pulsated within of its own accord. The rapture of bliss was steadily increasing. All those memories of the form of the supreme Blue Being, of His blessing, of His living within me, of my identification with Him, of "I am He"—all rang within me. I began to sway in the rapture of the sound of the *nada*, in the intensity of the love that spread through every part of my body, and in the memory of my fear of being destroyed by that divine Sphere of unmanifest light. There came more and deeper meditation, more profound experiences of the Self. Yet even then something inside me said that there was still further to go. I began to feel a lack of something, but there was nothing I could do about it. There was only one way to fill this lack: complete and unconditional surrender to the inner Shakti, who was Sri Gurudev. I went on meditating, and every day I saw that divine, radiant Sphere and the Blue Pearl inside it and heard the *nada* of the thunder. That was the state of my meditation.

Sometimes I would have fleeting visions of the all-knowing Blue Being, as quick as flashes of lightning. My meditation became deeper. Every day my conviction became stronger: "He is truly my inner Self, whose light is spread throughout the entire universe." Although I could not see it directly, I saw my inner Self as the Blue Person. Through the gift of Bhagavan Sri Nityananda's grace, I was gaining the realization that the Blue One was my own Self, the One who lives within all, pervades the entire universe and sets it in motion, who is one-without-a-second, nondual and undifferentiated, and yet is always at play, becoming many from one and one from many. He is Sri Krishna, the eternal Blue of Consciousness, the beloved life-breath of the *gopis*, and the Self of the yogis. This inner, eternal Blue of Consciousness is the *So'ham Brahma*—"I am He, the Absolute," of *jnanis*. This Blue is the adorable one chosen by *bhaktas*, who fills them with the nectar of love. This eternal Blue of Consciousness is Muktananda Swami's own beloved deity, Sri Guru Nityananda. This eternal Blue of Consciousness is the Siddha students' divine power of grace. If this is not realized, we cannot understand that the universe appears within God, the Absolute. But with the knowledge given to us by Parashakti Kundalini as She unfolds and grows within us, we can see the universe at play in the form of the Godhead.

I began to see that He, through whose grace *maya* becomes known as the manifestation of the Lord, is my Self appearing as the Blue Pearl. I began to see that the Blue One, whose light spreads through the whole world, the One from whom I received knowledge, who is the pure transcendent Witness of all, the unchanging Being, the unchanging Truth, is my inner Self. I became firmly established in the inner knowledge that just as the sun is visible and yet cannot be seen by the blind, in the same way, even though the Blue of Consciousness, the Witness of all, is apparent, it cannot be seen without the grace of the Guru. But a cloud cannot obscure the sun forever. He who reveals Himself for a moment and hides Himself for a moment, yet is revealed even when hidden, is my Self. I began to believe that He who takes care of my yogic *sadhana*, who was known to our ancestors, and who will be known to those who are to come, by whose grace our attachment to the world disappears, was my being, my consciousness, and my bliss. A firm and steadfast belief arose within me that that Blue One—who makes light shine, and who shines also in inert matter, without knowledge of whom all knowledge is incomplete, and with whose knowledge all things are easily known—was the form of the grace of Sri Guru Nityananda. And yet, while these convictions were becoming stronger, I had a subtle feeling that there was still a little more to go. The great Kundalini continually deepened my meditation and my knowledge of the Absolute. [Pp. 177–179]

My meditation was approaching its fulfillment. The end of my *sadhana*, the completion of my spiritual journey, the complete satisfaction of my Self, was coming near. The time had come for my Gurudev's command to be fulfilled. I was to reach the summit of man's fortune, which is divine realization. Once the vehicle of a spiritual traveler's *sadhana* has reached this point, it stops there forever. There, you may see nothing and hear nothing, but at the same time all is seen and heard, for inside you is the spontaneous conviction that you have attained everything. When an aspirant has reached there, he sits in bliss, sleeps in bliss, walks in bliss, comes and goes in bliss. He lives in an ashram in bliss, he eats in bliss; his behavior and actions are blissful. He experiences directly, "Now I have crossed the ocean of worldly existence." By virtue of this realization he is never agitated. No matter what he is doing, his heart is as calm as the ocean. All the afflictions of the mind melt away, and it becomes transmuted into Chiti. From inside comes the voice, "I am that which is dear to all, the Self of all, I am, I am." Now once again I saw Neeleshvara, the Blue Lord, whose nature is Satchidananda—Being, Consciousness, and Bliss. Seeing Him, the *sadhaka* enjoys happiness free from duality. He acquires supreme knowledge free from doubts, and knowledge of the identity of all things.

My very own, my dear Siddha students. My meditation was again as it had been earlier. From within, Bhagavan Nityananda seemed to shake me, and then the rays of the red aura lit up the 72,000 *nadis* and all the particles of blood. Immediately afterward the white flame stood before me, followed by her support, the black light, and finally my beloved Blue Pearl, the great ground of all. With the Blue Pearl my meditation immediately became more intense. My gaze turned upward. The Blue *bindu* of my two eyes became so powerful that it drew out the Blue Person hidden within the *brahmarandhra* in the middle of the upper *sahasrara* and placed Him before me. As I gazed at the tiny Blue Pearl, I saw it expand, spreading its radiance in all directions so that the whole sky and earth were illuminated by it. It was now no longer a Pearl but had become shining, blazing, infinite Light; the Light which the writers of the scriptures and those who have realized the Truth have called the divine Light of Chiti. The Light pervaded everywhere in the form of the universe. I saw the earth being born and expanding from the Light of Consciousness, just as one can see smoke rising from a fire. I could actually see the world within this conscious Light, and the Light within the world, like threads in a piece of cloth, and cloth in the threads. Just as a seed becomes a tree, with branches, leaves, flowers, and fruit, so within Her own being Chiti becomes animals, birds, germs, insects, gods, demons, men, and women. I could see this radiance of Consciousness, resplendent and utterly beautiful, silently pulsing as supreme ecstasy within me, outside me, above me, below me. I was meditating even though my eyes were open. Just as a man who is completely submerged in water can look around and say, "I am in the midst of water, I am surrounded on all sides by water; there is nothing else," so was I completely surrounded by the Light of Consciousness. In this condition the phenomenal world vanished and I saw only pure radiance. Just as one can see the infinite rays of the sun shimmering in all directions, so the Blue Light was sending out countless rays of divine radiance all about it.

I was no longer aware of the world around me. I was deep in divine feeling. And then, in the midst of the spreading blue rays, I saw Sri Gurudev, his hand raised in blessing. I saw my adored, my deity, Sri Nityananda. I looked again, and, instead, Lord Parashiva with his trident was standing there. He was so beautiful, so charming. He was made solely of blue light. Hands, feet, nails, head, hair were all pure blueness. As I watched, He changed, as Nityananda had changed, and now I could see Muktananda as I had seen him once before when I had had the vision of my own form. He too was within the Blue Light of Consciousness; his body, his shawl, his rosary of *rudraksha* seeds were all of the same blue. Then there was Shiva again, and after Shiva, Nityananda within the Blue. The Blue Light was still the same, with the sparkling luster of its rays and its wonderful blue color. How beautiful it was! Nityananda was standing in the midst of the shimmering radiance of pure Consciousness and then, as ice melts into water, as camphor evaporates into air, he merged into it. There was now just a mass of shining radiant Light with no name and form. Then all the rays bursting forth from the Blue Light contracted and returned into the Blue Pearl. The Blue Pearl was once again the size of a tiny lentil seed. The Pearl went to the place from where it had come, merging into the *sahasrara*. Merging into the *sahasrara*, Muktananda lost his consciousness, memory, distinctions of inner and outer, and the awareness of himself. Here I have not revealed a supreme secret because Gurudev does not command me to do so, God does not wish it, and the Siddhas do not instruct me to write it.

Now I went into inner *samadhi* and some time passed in this way. Then as Witness-consciousness began to return, the Blue Light appeared, which Shankaracharya describes as *sat chit neelima,* the eternal Blue of Consciousness. My meditation became focused on it. I began to experience that I was entering into the center of the *sahasrara* and the Blue Pearl, the support of all. As I passed inside the Blue Pearl, I once again saw the universe spreading out in all directions. I looked around everywhere and saw in all men and women—young and old, high and low, in each and every one—that same Blue Pearl that I had seen in myself. I saw that this was the inner Self within everyone's *sahasrara,* and with this full realization my meditation stopped, and I returned to normal body-consciousness. I still saw the Blue Pearl with my inner mind. It drew my attention toward itself, and as I looked at it, I attained peace and equanimity. My meditation continued like this every day.

I still meditate now, but I have a deep certainty that there is nothing more for me to see. When I meditate, the certainty that I have attained full realization fills me completely. I say this because of the three kinds of visions that I saw within the Blue Pearl and because in the outer world I still see that same Light of Consciousness, whose subtle, tranquil blue rays I had seen spreading everywhere after the three visions. It has never gone away. When I shut my eyes, I still see it shimmering and shining, softer than soft, more tender than tender, finer than fine. When the eyes are open, I see the blue rays all around. Whenever I see anyone, I see first the Blue Light and then the person. Whenever I see anything, I see first the beautiful subtle rays of Consciousness, and then the thing itself. Wherever my mind happens to turn, I see the world in the midst of this shining mass of Light. The way I see things, whether large or small, demonstrates the truth of the verses of Tukaram, which I have quoted before: "My eyes have been bathed with the lotion of the Blue Light, and I have been granted divine vision." [Pp. 182–185]

Even now when I meditate, as soon as I am absorbed in meditation, I see the mass of the blue rays of the Light of Consciousness and within that the Blue Pearl. I see this soft, gleaming Consciousness pulsating so delicately and shining in all my states. Whether I am eating or drinking or bathing it comes and stands before my eyes. Even when I am sleeping it is there. Now my vision is neither dual nor nondual, because that radiance is in both. There is no longer any demarcation between space, time, and substance. The Blue Light, subtly spreading everywhere, pervades my own being as it does the whole universe. I even see what is invisible. Just as with the lotion of mantras one can see an invisible and secret treasure, so the blue lotion, applied to my eyes by the grace of Sri Gurudev and the blessing of the divine Kundalini, has granted me divine realization, so that I can see that which is too subtle to be seen. Now I really know that my Self pervades everywhere as the universe. I am completely convinced that there is no such entity as the phenomenal world, that indeed there never was such an entity. What we call the universe is nothing other than the conscious play of Chiti Shakti. I have naturally and easily understood the significance of the *sah*, "He," and *aham*, "I," which combine to form *So'ham*. That knowledge described in Vedānta as "Thou are That," whose fruit is the bliss of the Absolute, is my very own Self gently vibrating within me. To confirm this I give an aphorism from the *Pratyabhijnahridayam*, which describes the viewpoint of Shiva, the supreme Self:

śrīmatparamaśivasya punaḥ viśvottīrṇa
viśvātmaka paramānandamaya
prakāśaikaghanasya evaṁvidhameva
śivādi dharaṇyantaṁ akhilaṁ
abhedenaiva sphurati na tu vastutaḥ
anyat kiṅchit grāhyam grāhakaṁ vā;
api tu śrīparamaśivabhattāraka eva itthaṁ
nānāvaichitryasahasraiḥ sphurati

This means that for Lord Parashiva, whom we also call Parameshvara and Parashakti, there is no such thing as the universe. He is true, eternal, attributeless, formless, all-pervasive, and perfect. He sees the whole universe, from Shiva to the earth—the moving and the unmoving, the manifest and the unmanifest—as supremely blissful Light, undifferentiated from Himself. There is nothing other than He; distinctions of seer and seen, subject and object, individual and universal, and matter and consciousness are not real. It is the vibrations of Lord Parashiva alone that produce the countless different forms of the universe. I see that the universe is the body of the Lord, and that Paramashiva Himself appears as the universe within His own being.

Jnaneshwar says in the last two verses of the poem that made me start writing *Chitshakti Vilas* [*Play of Consciousness*]:

> *tayāchā makaraṁda svarūpa teṁ śuddha brahmādikā*
> *bodha hāchī jhālā*
> *jñānadeva mhaṇe nivritti prasādeṁ nijarūpa*
> *govindeṁ janīm pāhatāṁ*

> The blissful essence of the Blue Lord which I have described here is the true nature of God. This has been the experience of all sages, from Brahma onward. My innermost form, envisioned by the favor of Sadguru Nivrittinath, is truly Govinda, the supreme Lord. I see Him everywhere. [Pp. 186–187]

Students of meditation know through experience that once their meditation becomes pure it becomes free from thought. For example, when your meditation is fixed on the Blue Pearl, the mind becomes permeated by it and, in fact, becomes it. You temporarily lose consciousness of yourself; you become oblivious of the inner and outer worlds: Objects are not seen when there is no one to see them, and sounds are not heard when there is no one to hear them. In that state there is neither happiness nor sorrow nor ignorance, neither perceiver nor perceived. Only the pure Paramatma, the supreme Self, remains, pulsating in His own being. It is an unwavering, thought-free, tranquil condition. It is the goal of your meditation. A man stays in this state for a short

> time, and then, when he begins to come out of meditation, he goes from *turiyatita* into the *turiya* state. Afterward, in *turiya*, no matter what happens, he will retain the realization of the transcendental state of *turiyatita*. Then, passing from *turiya* into *sushupti*, or deep sleep, he takes with him the experience of the *turiya* state. In deep sleep he still sees nothing different from himself. Leaving deep sleep and going into the dream state, he becomes his own dream world and all the objects of that state—chariots, horses, elephants, etc. He discovers that the Witness of the deep sleep state is the same as that of dreams. And then, passing from the dreaming to the waking state, he realizes that the same transcendental Being also underlies that. Thus from *turiyatita* to *turiya*, *turiya* to deep sleep, deep sleep to dreaming, dreaming to waking—and vice versa—only one Witness remains. The four states may differ from each other in various ways, but the Witness of them is the same. To become peaceful by understanding that there is one Witness of all the four states is, according to Muktananda, *sahajavastha*. [P. 265]

What is immediately apparent about the world created by Muktananda's meditations is that it is full of equals signs. One distinction after another is dissolved in favor of a more fundamental identity. "Who am I?" yields such answers as "I am Shiva," and "I am the Self." Images and qualities of the invariant reality that underlies everything emerge more and more in his meditation: the Light, the already attained Self, the unwavering joy. Variations in outer form are noted, but they do not become the basis of rigid categories. They merge. Shiva, Nityananda, and Muktananda are joined in one playful dance of appearances, and all are understood to be manifestations of the one radiant Light, the one Self.

The Direct Experience of Equality

These experiences clarify not only the world that is taking shape but also the one that is being left behind. The latter is the world of ignorance and illusion, in which we are continually being agitated by our perception of differences. In such a world, to be "different" always seems to imply either "better" or "worse." To be endlessly aware of differences leads to agonizing over the past and worrying about the future, since judgments and portents must be scanned for their implications. We insist on conjuring up a world of discrete entities locked in some inexorable chain of causality stretching back to a cosmic explosion and forward to the moment when our sun, having become a red nova, expands and engulfs the earth. In such a cosmology, there is no room for Intelligence, nor for Joy. There is room only for the congealing, combining, and eventual destruction of matter that is joined, perhaps, by some epiphenomenal consciousness that will eventually lose its necessary material support. In such a self-portrait, we appear to be short-lived creatures trapped in the fear that derives from our concern for individual identity, uniqueness, and predominance. To anyone caught in such a world, the universe is at most a stagnant extrusion of the divine, abandoned to its lawful but otherwise meaningless gyrations through time and space.

In contrast, the structure of consciousness that develops when primacy is given to universals and equality rather than to relative differences is the very basis of the intuition of the Self. What is the basis of that sameness? What is it that appears to be immanent in all these ten thousand things?

It seems helpful to find some name—God, the One, the Self—but names can confuse the issue. By naming the immanent "the One" or "the Self" we imply that it is an object, an entity hidden within the apparent. Thus, the fissure of difference and otherness reappears, and our thoughts slide back into the familiar but inaccurate forms of representation. We want to name it, but the result is always a betrayal of the experience of seamless unity between the apparent and the real. "The light is in me" is somehow a less satisfactory rendering of the experience than "I am the Light" or "I am Shiva." But even such equivalence statements represent a fading of the realization of identity in which the question of relationship does not even arise.

As each boundary becomes obsolete, all the energy that had been assigned to its preservation is released and made available. One unmistakable sign, therefore, of experiencing unity where previously there had been differences is the surge of relief, joy, and humor that accompanies the transformation in consciousness. The energy drain these distinctions create, and the fears that both lead to and flow from them, seem suddenly transformed into playful delight. One is on a permanent holiday from anxiety. The happiness that Muktananda conveys, in his narrative and in his everyday dealings with people, is the best refutation of any suspicion that the state of final realization might be boring. One merely loses one's fear, constriction, and the drain of energy that are inherent in the world of differences.

The Ego and the Self

We can give a more precise name to the process that is driven by a vigilant preoccupation with differences and to the structure formed by that process: *ahamkāra*. This Sanskrit term is usually translated as "ego," but since several quite different systems of thought employ this term, some caution is in order. As Muktananda writes, "Indian psychologists, the great sages who expounded *yoga*, understood that the mind takes four forms, each with a different function. When the mind is filled with thoughts, it is called *manas*. When it contemplates, it is called *chitta*. When it makes decisions, it is called *buddhi*, intellect. When it takes on the feeling of 'I'-ness, it is called *ahamkāra*, ego. Together, these four functions are called the *antahkarana*, or inner psychic instrument."[1]

Within psychoanalysis as developed by Freud and his followers, "ego" connotes maturity, the reality principle, the capacity to integrate conflicting tendencies such as impulses and internalized prohibitions. The ego is the hero of the story in successful psychoanalytic treatment and successful personality development. An ego that is strong, flexible, and still growing adaptively is highly desirable. Indian psychologists and sages certainly agree with psychoanalysis in valuing the capacity for accurate reality testing and the capacity to make decisions, but they would typically trace such capacities to the *buddhi* or intellect. They would describe someone whom psychoanalysis sees as having "a healthy ego" as having "a strong mind." They agree about this goal of human development, but they refer to it by different labels.

Finally, in popular parlance "ego" is often equated with conceit, presumptuousness, and a certain demanding childishness, as in the phrase, to have "a big ego." The Indian use of the term *ahamkāra*, however, is broader than this. Whereas "ego" popularly refers to self-inflation or narcissism, the workings of the *ahamkāra*, the ego, lead also to a seemingly modest, self-protective assessment of one's worth, tailored to avoid provoking the jealousy and retaliation of others.

From the Indian perspective, then, the ego underlies the experience of feeling small no less than the experience of feeling superior.

To recapitulate, in the Indian tradition, when the mind takes on the feeling of "I"-ness it is called *ahamkāra* or ego. Thus, "*ahamkāra*" connotes neither maturity nor conceit. It simply refers to a tendency to ask certain primary questions of life, to a way of scanning each situation to see: "How am I doing? How can I make myself less vulnerable? What are the potential sources of my pleasure and/or my pain? How can these people or this opportunity benefit me? How do I look? How do I compare with others?" From the Indian perspective, these questions we ask of each situation betray, and deepen, our delusion. They reveal the mind's habit of viewing everything from a limited, self-referent perspective. Henceforth, I will use the term ego to mean precisely this habit.

Muktananda reports that before his final meditative experiences he was inclined to answer the self-inquiry, "Who am I?" with the ego's familiar assertion: "I am this body." The tendency to draw boundaries and then determine our identity by comparing ourselves to others is reflected equally when we say, "I am this personality." The ego is the instrument of our desire for certainty and security, which we find in our identification with body and personality and in all the judgments that we use to define ourselves. Once we have fully identified ourselves with our body or with the contents of our mind, the ego's self-limiting assumptions underlie the whole range of self-appraisals. We make self-aggrandizing comparisons one day, while on the next we indulge in a protective form of self-effacement that offers the world no offense and hopes to attract no attention whatever. Our inevitably uneven reception in the world, taken by the ego as the measure of our value, throws us from hope to despair, from mania to deflation, and back again. The experience that derives from the ego's structuring of reality resembles the roller-coaster ride with its oscillation between highs and lows.

The contrast between the experience of the ego and that of the Self can be put in structural terms. In ordinary consciousness, each new experience, each other person, and even each known god must be located first with reference to oneself. "How do I feel about it?" "Does this person like me?" "How do I and my co-religionists think about that form of God?" The structure that forms under the aegis of the ego and its preoccupations is built on a series of comparisons, sharp edges, and well-maintained boundaries. This section of the Blue Pearl narrative shows, however, that the structure that forms from and yields the experience of the Self is sustained by a sense of commonality, identity, equality. The state of consciousness that arises from such a structure and sustains it is the state of true meditation. The meditative intuitions of oneness or of a fundamental void can replace the ego-dominated states of ordinary consciousness. The end result is called final realization, enlightenment, or sainthood. It is a state of being irrevocably beyond the ego. It is a state of adopting fully the perspective of the Self and of being totally identified with the Self. The saga of the Blue Pearl is thus the expression of a radical transformation in Muktananda's consciousness which is mirrored by successive waves of symbolic, visionary experience.

If Muktananda's earlier yogic and devotional meditations seemed utterly beyond one's own direct experiences, would it not be preposterous to search for personal parallels to his climactic moments of final realization? It might very well seem so, but then I must wonder: Did Muktananda tell his tale in order to elevate himself and deflate everyone else? What is he teaching by this narrative? Is it that he has attained the pinnacle, and I am either lost in the sleep of ignorance or else have barely begun the long upward climb? Or is it that I have surely had some inkling of true meditation, some inner opening to the Self, even if I have failed to recognize it? Clearly, the narrative presented in this chapter is intended to sustain the *jñānī*'s characteristic assertion: "There is, in fact, nothing to attain. The Self is already attained!" If that is the case, the least I can do is tentatively to accept the implication of this teaching that I differ from Muktananda more in what I recognize about myself than in what I am, in my very nature. Personal modesty or negation of my experience would amount to a blunt rejection of the teaching of the Blue Pearl narrative.

Explorations in Understanding

My experience, and that of many others within widely divergent cultural contexts, suggests that the first encounter with one's teacher contains in a highly condensed form numerous glimpses of the journey that lies ahead. Remarkable realizations burst into consciousness in those early days. More understandings than can possibly be absorbed flood the system. It seems, then and later, that one has been given a prospectus for a radically altered perception of reality which may take years to become fully operative. This rush of yogic experience, feelings of devotion, and new understandings is at once disorienting and a delicious promise of what one may come to integrate in a calmer, less frantic time.

I recall a questionnaire that I was asked to complete during Muktananda's second week in Ann Arbor. One of the questions was, "What are your main interests?" I answered, "Peace." One of my major preoccupations, then and during the ten previous years of the Vietnam era, was the anti-war movement. But my answer was also prompted by hints of an inner peace I had experienced after being around Muktananda. Even on the day I had met him, though I was crushed because I thought he hadn't seen the Blue Pearl in me, I had slipped into some layer of deep peace and soft darkness.

Although it is true that the inner tumult of thoughts and physical pain made some of my efforts at meditation seem completely fruitless, and some meditations seemed inadequate because nothing seemed to happen, other meditations were remarkable precisely because "nothing" happened. Those were the times when I reentered that layer of peace and contentedness. Still, my early inklings of the inner realm were not enough to prevent me from wondering, several years later, if my characteristic "black nothing" experience in meditation was proof that I was doing something wrong or that meditation was losing its value for me. It was during one period of such wondering that the blackness in meditation became even blacker, even more intense. The field of blackness suddenly was broken by an uneven area of red hot and white hot fire. Apparently, a small piece of the wall of a huge blast furnace had fallen away. All along, I realized, the blackness had been merely the outer covering signifying containment but not diminution of the inner process, the inner fire. There was a peaceful blackness, and there was an infinite reservoir of energy and power within the blackness, and both realities seemed to be equally valid portraits of my inner Self.

What impresses me about these early events is how many of them taught me something about the world of differences and about equality. In 1974 I would have been most likely to answer the question "Who am I?" with the then current phrase, "I am a political person." I had been very involved in the anti-war movement: the teach-ins, door-to-door campaigns, protest marches, huge rallies, and, that year, the Indochina Peace Campaign. These efforts, and the movement for civil rights and against racism, had been central to my life for fifteen years.

My understanding of the world of differences and the possibility of attaining equal vision was deeply affected by the following events, which took place during Muktananda's stay in Ann Arbor. As the lovely autumn days went by, I found that I was spending more and more time at the ashram during Muktananda's visit. I began to tell others about the amazing world of chanting and incense and the delightful, charismatic man at the center of it all. In one of my classes, which was composed of some of the few students still involved in social change, I announced that the ashram was having a *saptah*, a dancing chant, in the basement of the Friend's Meeting House and asked if anyone wanted to attend. Most did, and we agreed to meet there and see what it was all about.

The first event was not, as I had expected, a dancing chant. Instead, Amma, one of Muktananda's oldest devotees, showed a few silent 8-mm reels of Muktananda in India. In the first scenes, we watched endless lines of devotees file past Muktananda's chair during his birthday celebration, each devotee adding something to the mountain of gifts. As she narrated, Amma duly noted each VIP, each minister of state, each chief justice. I didn't like what I saw, and the next scenes only made things worse. Row upon row of villagers—I called them peasants in my mind—were awaiting and then receiving gifts of food and clothing from Muktananda. My perspective became totally that of the leftist, and I judged the entire proceedings to be a classic example of feudalism. I was rapidly filling up with political rage. In China, I thought, there would be neither such wealth nor such charitable dispensations. The movie had left me completely alienated from the Indian social structure and, above all, anything to do with Muktananda. There was certainly no point in staying for the *saptah*. Nor could I imagine attending the weekend retreat only two days away. I felt embarrassed about having subjected the students to such political backwardness, and all I could think to do was leave, immediately. As the music for the *saptah* started, I dashed up the stairs, thinking, "Well, that's it. It's been interesting, but that's it."

Later that night, having gone to bed in roughly the same mood, I had an unusually vivid and memorable dream. I was standing in the huge living room of what I took to be my house, although it actually resembled the home of a senior member of my Department. Overlooking a river lined with weeping willows, the house had many glass windows, from floor to ceiling. It was getting dark, and I could see quite a few car headlights approaching. People were parking at the turnaround and walking in a steady procession up the path to the house. They seemed to be arriving for a meeting, but what meeting? What was the occasion?

As the living room began to fill up with people standing in small groups, I drifted from conversation to conversation trying to figure out who these people were and why they had come. At first, I kept hearing phrases like "school system change," and so I concluded, "Oh, these are Jean's people. They're here for a meeting of her project." My wife had been working on issues of educational change over the previous ten years and was at that time employed as a mental health consultant to the local school system. I relaxed. It was clear what was going on.

But then someone set up a movie screen at one end of the room. There was a bustle of chairs being rearranged. I circulated among the visitors again and learned that they intended to show a movie on the life of Mao. "Oh," I thought, "these must be Marilyn's people." Marilyn was a university colleague, a fellow radical, and an expert on modern China.

As the chairs and couches were being arranged into a circle around the screen, I saw my youngest son pushing the couch that would close the circle. I also noticed, as apparently he did not, that on the floor, just where the couch was to be located, sat a dark-skinned Indian man in an orange *lungi* and shawl. It was Muktananda. He seemed completely composed and relaxed. Instantly, the rage of the previous afternoon returned, and I heard myself saying clearly: "That's right, Davey, run him over."

The scene immediately vanished. I found myself sitting face-to-face with Swami Muktananda. We appeared to be in an analyst's office. He was the analyst, and I the analysand. I was recounting, slowly and carefully, the sequence that had just taken place in the living room. When I had finished with my injunction that my son run him over, I paused. It was the pause of the analysand who hopes for some response, some interpretation, despite the overwhelming odds against getting even one word in reply. But this analyst responded: "Well, it appears that you have quite a problem about being the host."

In the dream, I reeled from the accuracy, power, and implications of Muktananda's interpretation. I was convinced that I had never received such an insightful summary not only of a dream but of my whole facilitative stance in life. I was so impressed with this swami-analyst that I decided to confront him with what seemed to be my most urgent question. I held up my hands, partially as a taunt and partially as a plea. In one hand was the bright yellow Beacon Press edition of Gandhi's autobiography; in the other was Schram's biography of Mao. In effect, I was asking, "Which one?" As I sat there with Muktananda's face framed by the two books, my arms were gradually being pressed together by an irresistible force. At last, the two books converged into one, and the result was an explosion of white light and jolts of energy coursing through my body.

As I hovered between the dream and wakefulness, I heard Amma say to me, "Well, what did you think he was, god of the radicals?" In the torrent of thoughts that followed, I realized first that all of my alienation and rage were completely gone. I also realized that yes, of course, I had hoped, assumed, demanded that he be a radical. He had to be on my team. But as Amma's voice and the film returned to my mind, it dawned on me that Amma had portrayed *her* Muktananda in the film. It was *her* portrait of *her* guru. My situation became quite clear. I had a choice to make. I could insist that Muktananda be a radical, like me and my gang. I could be furious that he was embroiled with status-conscious reactionaries. Or I could be thoroughly relieved that he made no invidious distinctions among people, VIPs or peasants, and was simply available to everyone. That struck me as the only way for a god, a guru, or an analyst, to be. He was not there to represent or to be monopolized by one faction or another.

Obviously, however, I was. Muktananda's interpretation, as I mulled it over, applied not only to the confused, off-balance character in the early section of the dream. It applied to me; my "problem about being the host" was so acute that I had been totally preoccupied with what my radical students were thinking about the movie. The irony of the situation was that, although I had left in a rage, the students had stayed on, having found the movie interesting and the *saptah* wonderful. I realized, as the dream faded, that the host who is owned by his guests, or captured by his construction of what his guests are thinking, was precisely the kind of person I did not want to be any longer. In fact, I decided, if life around Muktananda was going to be anywhere near as therapeutic as that dream had been, maybe I had better go to the weekend retreat after all.

The dream was an initiation into the world beyond differences, the world of unity and fearlessness, and the great relief associated with its discovery. The political person I had become was so preoccupied with the differences between factions, lines, "good guys" and "bad guys" and between such words as feudalism and socialism that the goal of peace, inner or outer, was becoming less and less attainable. If all perceptions of the fundamental unity of people and approaches are deemed incorrect, backward tendencies, then the mind will work mainly to defend "us" and denigrate "them." In the dream I had asked the analyst-teacher to choose between two books, two paths, and the explosive answer had been, "Understand that they are the same."

Spirituality and Politics

I am not writing a commentary on political life or on the campaigns for freedom, dignity, and justice. I know and admire scores of political people who have, as far as I can see, no need to begin exploring the issues I had to confront in those days because they are already doing so. I am writing about myself, about one person at one moment in recent history. As I reviewed my life at that time, a long-suppressed awareness could no longer be restrained. My companions and I may have been pursuing goals of peace, mutual respect, and equality on the vast canvas of national and global politics, but we were actually moving away from these goals in our immediate lives, year by year. The ways in which we first condoned and then trapped ourselves in the mounting violence of those days could no longer be ignored—nor could the disparity between the goal of genuine community and the actual fragmentation and mutual recrimination among the few remaining activists.

Our values, our ideals, and our sense that those in power were leading us in terrible directions had gotten us moving, but there was something missing. The clearest indication of that missing element was, for me, bound up with the Blue Pearl. When Muktananda writes, "I looked around everywhere and saw in all men and women—young and old, high and low, in each and every one—that same Blue Pearl that I had seen in myself," he is describing the direct experience of equality.

I had been pursuing the goal of equality, but what was the nature of my daily experience? Did I really see with equal vision or was I trying to rearrange the world that I blamed for "forcing" me to accept its unequal arrangements and perceptions? Without a deep sense of the equality of all people, I was left with a vague, ineffectual commitment to a goal. Equality, in those days, was something granted only conditionally, only to "our side," to those with whom we empathized, or to our allies of the week or month. I sometimes wonder at the length of time it took us to realize that we were slowly yielding to all the habits of mind and temper that we thought characterized only the "bad guys": arrogance, self-indulgence, and a mounting rage at the enemy, the unconvinced, and our closest rivals, to name but a few.

It is possible, without losing for a moment the inner sense of equality, to act compassionately toward people in need and even to thwart those who plunder the lives and property of others. The direct experience of equality, symbolized for Muktananda by his vision of the Blue Pearl in everyone and expressed by him in his daily dealings with people thereafter, is the highest meditation and the fruit of the completed spiritual journey. However, the journey takes place in stages. As a start, we can turn away from blind alleys and give up destructive habits and counter-productive polarizations. My dream sequence suggested that I could, if I chose to, see the commonality between Gandhi and Mao, just as Muktananda could see the commonality between us radicals and the VIPs of traditional Indian society.

Our bravado, wildly optimistic predictions, and huddling together against the storm during all those political years had done nothing to reduce our fear. If anything, it became greater each year. And yet here was a human being living in a state of equal vision, and, among other things, he was an amazing example of fearlessness. No one can harm a person who understands death and who sees the same Self in himself and each person he greets. He cannot be hurt by criticism, nor does he consider anyone to be of lesser value than himself, expendable, or the hated enemy. If equal vision between physical life and physical death, between the apparent me and the apparent other, and between all others is attained, the personal goal of peace and contentment is reached. It is not contingent on the structure of one's society or personal life because the understanding that underlies it leads directly to unconditional equanimity.

In contrast, the political life I had known went beyond the healthy and necessary distinction-making capacity of the mind. It went beyond the simple awareness of what is useful to the world versus what is destructive to it. It forged a thoroughgoing dualism in which the Prince of Darkness, in modern guise, reigned with an unremitting and immense power. What was the source of this vision of reality? Might it not have been a projection of that part of our own consciousness that is anchored not in the Self but in the ego's terror-filled world of differences and mistrustful, separative relations among people? I have no doubt that there is real cruelty and injustice in the world, but this fact can become the pretext for us to activate the familiar dualisms of our own immature inner world. Thus, when we project the negative side of our good guy versus bad guy dualism onto a convenient target, we leave ourselves wide open to the experience of hatred, dehumanizing attributions of evil motivation, and undisciplined violence of thought and action. Such a world view is born of fear and vigilance and leads to more of the same. Thus, political life can become one round after another of schism, recrimination, and isolation.

The dream brought to the surface of my awareness the possibility of moving in another direction. Perhaps I could base my thoughts and actions on my own life experience, rather than on the frail, ideological commitments that had failed to block the downward spiral. Perhaps I could reorient my life around the values inherent in the moments of equanimity. But any such shift could only come gradually. I needed to see that equal vision didn't mean blurred vision—an inability to distinguish between kindness and cruelty, justice and greed. I needed to see, as eventually I did see in the person of Muktananda, that the equality revealed by the omnipresence of the Blue Pearl did not preclude the highest standards of personal and societal conduct.

I have not reached some final plateau of political awareness and effectiveness. However, I have found, from watching Muktananda and those who have learned much of what he has to teach, that it is possible to lead one's life in a state of pure love and respect for others regardless of the current political or economic arrangements of one's society. Beneath their interaction and specific gestures, I see in operation an understanding that resonates with Muktananda's experiences with the Blue Pearl.

I recall several occasions in Muktananda's large ashram in Oakland. On three successive days my wife and I had been able to attend "private *darshan*," during which about twenty people would approach Muktananda, one or two at a time, with some personal or difficult question. I sat, for most of these periods, just a few feet to the side of his chair. I could hear the questions, the translation, and his response. Each person would approach Muktananda in a state of pain and uncertainty, and he would respond with an indescribable gesture of availability and warmth. He would answer the questions as soon as they were translated, with delicacy and support, but with no tentativeness. What struck me even more was the effect his response would have on the questioners. They would seem startled, delighted, reassured, amazed, and relieved, all at the same time. And yet Muktananda seemed to be exerting no effort to size up the questioner, ponder the situation, or formulate a reply. He seemed totally engaged, sharing the questioner's sense of the importance of the moment. Still, as far as I could tell, he wasn't thinking at all, at least not in the way I understood the process. He seemed to be "on automatic," completely relaxed, content, and confident. I had never seen anything remotely like it.

I gradually concluded that the people who approached him, whether they came for advice, for blessing, for direction, or merely out of curiosity, came equipped with an inner voice that they could not hear. He could, however, and did. Somehow, not only could Muktananda hear the voice, but he was willing to let it resonate through his own voice and gesture. He seemed to just sit there, perfectly content to be the vehicle by which people might have a momentary encounter with their own inner voice, their own inner Self. Only in this way could I account for the delight, the surprise, and the relaxation of those whose brief *darshan* with him I had observed. It was as if something in Muktananda's answer conveyed the intimacy, the knowledge of one's hidden thoughts, that one associates with being in touch with one's deepest, truest self. The impasse at which these people had arrived seemed to vanish under the impact of the primary message in his response, which was, "You are known." Suddenly, their fear and isolation and bitterness were undercut by the response of this stranger from India. However, for that to happen, the voice they were hearing had to be their own, whether or not they recognized it as such.

Every once in a while, as I sat there, I would try to view the situation from Muktananda's perspective, and I would have an inkling of his realization that the same Self, the same Blue Pearl, blazed in every person he met. There was, in that realization, no hint of separation or otherness—and no fear. He "knew" the answers that the inner voice of the person before him would give to the question or problem that had been posed. It was as if Muktananda could point each person to his own Self because some recognizable manifestation of the one Self, the Self of all, was available to him, moving through him without any effort on his part. If asked to account for what he was doing and how he was doing it, he might simply point at the picture of his guru, Nityananda, and say, "He's doing everything."

I found a point of convergence between Mao and Gandhi, between politics and spirituality, in that scene in Oakland. What more powerful way to resolve the many questions and problems that beset the world than for everyone to gain access to his own authentic, wise, and loving voice? How could the structures of consciousness that sustain, on the one hand, depression and passivity or, on the other, greed, violence, and injustice—structures, in either case, that are filled with fear—survive in either the victim or the victimizer if the voice of the inner Self were fully available to each person?

I could see in a new light why Muktananda was constantly giving food and shelter to the *adivasis*, the tribal people of his district in Maharashtra, India. Of course, he gave—food, medical care, love, understanding—whatever each person needed to survive and grow and realize the Self. However, I could also see why he gave and taught and made himself endlessly available to the wealthy and the powerful as well. His welcoming *all* people was nothing but an expression of his understanding, and that in turn was nothing but a pure distillation of his own experience of the Self in himself and in "all men and women—young and old, high and low, in each and every one."

The Ego and the Process of Self-Inquiry

As I recall the personal experiences that seem to be connected with the path of understanding, I am struck by how often they convey a teaching about the nature of the ego. My momentary intuitions of the meditative state, the state of unity and the Self, interrupted the otherwise constant operation of my ego. Self-consciousness and self-protectiveness refer not to the experience of the Self but to my ego's limited sense of my true identity.

If, during meditation, my mind is filled with judgments about my inability to "really meditate," it is the ego at work. At such times, I wonder if some skeptical, ill-wishing, and fault-finding person has taken up residence in my self-appraisal system. It is odd that my ego's preoccupation with the quality of my meditation should manifest in the form of an inner voice that seems so alien and unsympathetic. The voice appears to be the result of internalizing the message of some other person, now far removed in space and time, someone whose own ego is expressed by the invidious comparisons at my expense. Where does that voice come from?

If my response to a movie about Swami Muktananda is being distorted by an intense concern with the opinion that my fellow radicals or my activist students will have about the movie, then it is the ego that has taken over. It is the ego that is busy anticipating future trouble, that is imagining that the others will turn on me and ask, "Do you mean that you just sat there and enjoyed that spectacle on the screen? You didn't see it as decadent feudalism?" Without the ego's characteristic concern for what others might think of me, who knows how I might have reacted to the movie? The ego manifests as voices that somehow have become internalized and powerful.

If, in my dream, strangers are crowding into my living room and out of anxiety I drift from conversation to conversation trying to figure out what is happening, is that not a portrait of the process of self-negation by which the ego is formed? I am being invaded, but I continue to play the role of the "good host." By turning myself over to these people, my ego is fearfully trying its best to avoid being left out or criticized. In the process, however, the would-be critics, the radicals of the dream who are stand-ins for the radicals of the previous day, become the basis of the inner voice that urges my son to run over the swami with the couch. In the next part of the dream I use the swami as an analyst, and in describing the scenario I open myself up for his interpretation of my "host problem." Only then do the internalized others lose their hold on me, allowing me to turn to yet another version of the same struggle: the choice between Gandhi and Mao. The merging of the two books and the resulting explosion, the liberation of energy and the experience of freedom, are the results of moving beyond the ego's structure of introjected factions whose opinion of me I fear.

The structure that emerges from the dream, stripped now of any invidious comparisons between factions or paths, is far less dominated by the anxiety that produces and feeds the ego. The new structure is far closer to the Self in its direct experiencing of equality and the unity that underlies apparent diversity. The finale of the dream, in which Amma's voice ("Well, what did you think he was, god of the radicals?") exposes my need to make certain that Muktananda is on my side of the political fence, represents the sharpest blow at the ego. As I awoke, I realized that he wasn't on my side or on any side, and my appreciation of Muktananda's teachings on equality was expressed by a great surge of relief and happiness.

The ego is responsible for compounding our sense of bounded separateness. Through the processes of memory, identification, and internalization, we come to mistake voices from the past, our own and those of many others, for our authentic voice of the current moment. Our fearful accommodations and conformity to significant others leave behind a residue that becomes the nucleus of the ego. In order to preserve or advance the cause of this isolated, vulnerable entity that we consider ourselves to be, we perform a most peculiar act. While sharpening the differences between ourselves and the others we fear, we also store their voices, their judgmental commentaries, within us. Then we proceed to identify with these internal judgments as if they were our own. We do the same with praise, whether it is accurate and helpful or merely represents how someone wishes we were or wishes we would see ourselves.

Our difficulties begin when these voices set in motion the see-saw of unstable self-esteem and intensify our assumptions of separateness, conditional value, and vulnerability to assessment. The ego is a system of assumptions and concerns that can become increasingly impervious to change. However, it is the collision of the ego with the experience of the divine, of the benign Other, and of the Self that yields the moment of freedom and lightness. As the structure of the ego loosens, sometimes the liberated moment can stretch into permanent transformation. What happens then?

Even if the Self is glimpsed for only a moment, two intuitions that are not easily assimilated may begin to take shape. The first takes the intuitive perception of nondifferentiation and identity straight to its obvious conclusion: "Well, then, I am God." The second finds the constants of the Self, the joy, radiance, and beauty, everywhere, always: "The world is perfect, as it is." In short, if one's intuitions of the highest states of meditation can stabilize and become permanent, the result is a mode of being in the world that I was raised to consider impossible to attain and illegitimate to claim or even desire.

As we attempt to understand these two verbal assertions, "I am God" and "The world is perfect," our attitude toward them is what is most important. If we are firmly rooted in the logic and assumptions of ordinary consciousness, then naturally we react to them in the age-old way. We don't feel that we are divine, and we don't see everything as perfect, so how can anyone else? A sentence such as "I am God" seems to imply that the speaker thinks only he is God. The speaker seems to be arrogantly disparaging the rest of us mortals. We are inclined to think of God as an object, or as the single occupant of some high office. Therefore, the only people who would assert "I am God" must be pretenders, false messiahs, or the deluded. It cannot be true. But what if this response is based on only one of many possible sets of assumptions, logic, and truths?

The assertions "I am God" and "The world is perfect" may be viewed as teachings of the path of *jnāna* or understanding that derive from a deep state of meditation.[2] The teacher's intention is to convey the meaning of his own experience to the seeker not through verbalizations but by actually giving the seeker the experience itself. The meditative state leads one to define a person not by contrasts but by what one can sense through intuition as the essential quality inherent in everyone. No one is disparaged, and no one is exalted as the only example of divinity, because the experience of difference has been reduced to a very minor aspect of reality. Awareness of the ground of all existence and the immanence of the divine in everything is the fruit of a radically different attitude toward oneself and the world.

Another key to the experience of the Self in meditation is found in the Blue Pearl narrative. Up to a certain point Muktananda considered the Blue Pearl to be an object, the fourth body, the inner Other, the gift of the Goddess. Then it appeared to be the vehicle of the Blue Person, the indwelling Lord, or the sphere of unmanifest Light. However, Muktananda's feeling of incompleteness, his conviction that there was "still further to go," did not leave him until he himself entered the Blue Pearl. Only when he felt himself to be located at the center of the Blue Pearl and experienced the universe radiating out from that absolute point of reference was the journey complete. To identify oneself fully with the unmanifest Light, the void, or the matrix from which all creation arises is to have the direct experience that any verbal assertion, such as "I am God," can only approximate. Since everything is born from that Center and is filled with its radiance, it naturally follows that whatever exists is perfect and all perceptions that suggest otherwise address secondary aspects of the manifest universe.

Meditation and Self-Esteem

Muktananda uses these Blue Pearl experiences as the basis of his central teachings: "Honor yourself. Kneel to yourself. Worship yourself. Your God dwells within you as you." And, equally: "Welcome others with respect and love. See God in each other. Make this your daily worship." This twofold teaching is an invitation to meditate, to explore that inner state from which affirmations of one's true identity and one's true relationship to others flow in a perfectly natural way.

The more I have pondered these teachings, the more they have become a tantalizing kaleidoscope, shifting from one meaning to another. Sometimes the meanings seem to clash with one another. Sometimes they seem to fit into one coherent perspective. My first interpretation was that I should try to see beneath the surface of who I appear to be and recognize an Inner Self. This, I told myself, was my essence, my divinity. But was that "the" Inner Self or "my" Inner Self? In what sense could it be "mine" if it was universal or divine? The dilemma I had created for myself derived from my equation of

Self with soul, an inner spark which I "housed" but could not possibly call my own.

My second interpretation was the result of a casual conversation I had with a friend whose native language is Hindi. He pointed out that Muktananda's actual phrases could convey, for an Indian, quite a different message. It could easily be taken to mean what in English would be translated as, "Honor yourself." The phrase, *āpko vando*, could be taken to mean, "Kneel to yourself," and *āpko dhyāo*, "Meditate on yourself." What could that mean? It seemed that he was deliberately inviting us to honor ourselves and each other just as we are.

When the opportunity arose, I asked Amma, who was by then known as Swami Prajnananda, why Muktananda used such an informal, colloquial manner in referring to the Self. "Why doesn't he use the term *ātman*?" I wondered. "That would seem more scriptural," I said, "because it would be translated as, 'Honor the Self.'" Her answer was immediate: "Because Baba knows that the greatest obstacle to our spiritual progress is our tendency to put ourselves down, and that is why he urges us, over and over again, to think highly of ourselves." She then reminded me that Muktananda was fond of repeating, "Never say to yourself, 'I am small. I am a sinner. I am weak.' Say instead, 'I am great. I am divine.'"

For a long time, I could only slide back and forth between two perspectives. One suggested honoring a hidden or latent glory, the Self. The other maintained that even our current state is worthy of being honored. The ambiguity and the potential paradox turn out to be embedded in the Sanskrit language and its modern forms, including Hindi and Marathi. The word *ātman* is not used for only metaphysical discussion. Its use ranges all the way from the ineffable Brahman, the ultimate reality, to the ordinary, everyday sense of "oneself." It shares a common root with the second person pronoun (*āp*) that Muktananda uses in his teachings. The ambiguity turns out to be an essential part of the teaching. The Sanskrit language encourages a prolonged meditation on where, if anywhere, we should draw the line between sacred and profane, divine and ordinary, Self and self.

One further interpretation has overtaken my internal debate. It rejects the implicit assumption of the controversy: that what we should honor can be thought of as if it were an object. It goes beyond the valuation of an aspect of ourselves, as object, to the location of ourselves as subject. Honoring the Inner Self and honoring ourselves as we are converge when we understand our true nature as subject, awareness, consciousness.

It is not that our ordinary self is one rather pathetic thing but our Inner Self is another quite wonderful thing. The Self is not an object. Nor is it that we should honor ourselves, just as we are, because we have nothing to learn and no growth ahead of us. Rather, it is in our status as subject, as Witness or Experiencer, that we are "the" Self, "our" Self, and "truly ourself." But the truth of the matter is that we do turn ourselves into objects. We don't identify ourselves as the Witness of our thoughts, nor as the unwavering light of consciousness, the Self. And to the extent that we do not identify ourselves as the subject of our universe, we do indeed have a long way to go. There is, however, every reason for one who has "attained the Self" to honor us, as we are *and* as the Self. The distinction between the limited form and the absolute is no longer a final one. When Muktananda reports that he sees the Blue Pearl in each person he meets, no less than in himself, he is describing the state of the self-realized being.

Our yearning to reverse the deeply ingrained habits of doubting and belittling ourselves sets in motion the process of transformation. We search for some way to abandon, if only for a moment, the structure of consciousness that breeds comparisons and self-denigrations. The experience of meditation provides us with some respite from the workings of the ego.

An incident that showed me many of the important contrasts between ego and Self, between ordinary consciousness and meditation, took place in 1975. At the beginning of a ten-day stay in the Oakland ashram I attended an Intensive. This weekend program, designed as an introduction to meditation, included several talks on the theory of meditation and *yoga*.

I was happy to be there. I was feeling an unexpected but satisfying sense of having returned home. The ashram seemed magical and beautifully arranged. But, faster than I could have imagined, the pendulum of my emotions swung in the other direction.

One of the first talks was about the esoteric Indian teaching concerning Kundalinī, the subtle body, *chakra*s, and auras. I winced inside as the talk began. These esoteric topics were hardly my favorite aspect of Siddha Yoga. I tried to maintain an attitude of interest and openmindedness, but when the speaker began to assert that auras were evidence of the subtle body, that the Kundalinī power rose higher and higher through the *chakras*, and that each *chakra* had a certain color and a certain number of petals, I lost my composure. For one thing, I kept thinking, "What if my colleagues in psychology could see me now, listening to all this mumbo-jumbo!" For another, the speaker wasn't relating most of her assertions to anything she herself had experienced. Each new detail of yogic anatomy seemed to be introduced by, "They say . . . . " Who were "they?" In my mounting anger, scorn, and mistrust, I began to mumble to myself, "Does everyone have to believe all this? Do I have to? This is just dogma. Am I the only one in the room who thinks this is ridiculous?"

The crescendo of inner turmoil was reaching the breaking point when, from some previously ignored part of myself, a voice said, "Look at the state you're in right now." And the implication was, "What are you going to do about it?" In the midst of this bitterness and anger there was just enough energy to bring out of my depths what I would later call my first authentic prayer: "Help!" This unvocalized but desperate plea was aimed at Baba Muktananda, and I managed to repeat it several times. But before long I was pulled back into a morass of self-pity: "Why did I come all this way? Why did I spend all that money on air fare?" Meanwhile, the speaker was plodding through her diagrams and her "They say's."

Suddenly I noticed that there was a layer of air just below the ceiling that looked like the brownish smog that often hangs over Mexico City. As I watched this smog settling lower and lower in the room, it reached eye level, and I had to duck under it to see the speaker clearly. Eventually, it reached the floor and filled the entire room. I could barely make out the speaker in the front of the room, but, more significantly, I couldn't hear anything she was saying. I could see her mouth forming words. I could see the attentive audience. But I was enveloped by an unimaginably soft, quiet, and peaceful atmosphere. The last echoes of all my rage and rejoinder simply faded away, and in their place was nothing—nothing, that is, except first a ripple and then a tidal wave of sheer delight. I sat there feeling like the Cheshire cat, all grin and no thought. I continued to watch the speaker and the people around me but I had no reaction to any of it. After a while the speaker sat down, the people noiselessly clapped their hands, the fog lifted, and I sat there in a state of serene wonder. My first thought was, "I guess prayers do get answered." But even that conclusion, novel though it was to me, seemed to evoke very little thought and emotion.

What does all of this have to do with the ego and meditation? Many aspects of the ego's structure of consciousness are at play here. First, I see the introjected others, the reference group of colleagues. They are in me. They are the source of that primal threat that can exist all one's life. The threat, in one form, is this: "You can associate with those people if you like, but if you do, don't think that you can come back to us, ever again. It's your decision." The ego forces choices and creates showdowns. I stand at the threshold of something new, but the threat from the old is too powerful. I don't dare jeopardize the ties to those who threaten me, and so I not only hesitate, I fall in with "their" assessment. I see through their eyes, which makes me their prisoner. In making a concession to these internalized opinions and pressures, I have reduced myself to someone who could not survive "their" rejection, scorn, and ostracism.

The ego, responsible for my internal compliance with my colleagues and my externalized scorn for the speaker, was thwarting my efforts to accomplish what I had traveled all the way to Oakland to do—to break its grip and gain access to the state of meditation. My anger at the speaker and at all the "docile" listeners betrayed a yearning to break through into a state where some unfettered self would emerge. I wanted to share not their apparent acquiescence but their playful enjoyment of this strange, esoteric lecture. Frozen though I was at the threshold, it conveyed to me the yogic teaching that I could and should step out of the way of the process of my own self-transformation. The attribution of that process to the Kundalinī or to changes in the subtle body was not the primary message. The main point was that my life task was not one of courting approval but of allowing a more authentic level of myself than I had ever known to purify me and take over one aspect of my life after another. But I couldn't defy the threat. All that I could do was pray, call for help, and wait.

In retrospect, the answer to my prayer doesn't represent any model for negotiating all such ego crises. I have never again prayed for help with such desperation, nor have I found rooms filling up, or down, with brown smog. But it did happen once, and I must say that the message had a great impact on me. It taught me the consequences of letting go of the ego, of letting its characteristic preoccupations slide by. It taught me about the welling up of joy and peace that comes from not clinging so tightly to the internalized cast of characters in my ego's web. If that contentment and centeredness, that outpouring of the Self, is available inside, how seriously can I take any conditional threat, internal or external? Placating these internalized, ghostly voices can provide occasional respite from the menace of exclusion and scorn, but nothing can compare with tapping the source of unconditional, self-born contentment.

The experience of the Self in that meditative smog remains the significant core of that event. I still do not bring many of the esoteric formulations into my ordinary professional mode of functioning. I still don't believe in *chakras* and auras in the way that the speaker seemed to, but I have had the sort of meditative experiences that underlie such intuitive formulations. Actually, these esoteric ideas are valuable to me because they are an expression of people's meditative intuitions and thus open up communication between us. I am impelled not to quarrel with them but, instead, to turn within and locate my own parallel experiences and share these in terms with which I feel comfortable.

Different readers will take different routes to explore the meaning of Muktananda's account of final realization. They will at different times conclude, "Now I have a way of thinking about how Muktananda's experiences might apply to me and my own spiritual journey." I am particularly fascinated by Muktananda's awareness of being at the center of the universe. The resulting assertion, "I am God," is the last of a series of intuitions that I can share, not through replicating the specific content of Muktananda's visionary meditations, but through exploring their implications for me. What they seem to imply for him, and what they certainly imply for me is this: "I make the universe. The universe is more than a purely physical or mental system. It is consciousness. It is a system of meaning of which I am the creator, sustainer, and destroyer." They imply to me, "I do not need to identify with the apparently fixed elements of my life, my body, my life history, my personality. I may identify with, I may recognize my unity with, the deeper process of awareness itself. Something endures in the midst of everything. It is consciousness, and I am that. The world of differences is the play of that consciousness, and I affirm my identity with that play because from the center, where I locate myself, all meaning arises." What this implies about those around me is essentially the same: We are all epicenters of the one conscious energy, and we are each the creators of our own meaning and experience.

The Emerging Synthesis

From the vantage point of the final section of the Blue Pearl narrative, we can see more clearly than when we began the sequential phases of Muktananda's journey. First, the themes of power and purification emerged, then the fullness of devotion, and finally the understanding called the realization of the Self. The phases are distinguishably different from each other, but it is also true that each meditative vision contains elements of all three themes. The three segments point not to a set of mutually exclusive categories or spiritual paths but to a progression that is highly complex.

The sequential order of Muktananda's experiences reveals a progressively more inclusive integration of themes rather than a superceding of all previous themes by the subsequent one. The result is an evolving synthesis, and I construe Muktananda's teaching to be not that these thematic elements must emerge in the order they did for him but that they must all be fully present before the transformative process is complete.

From the beginning to the end, the complex synthesis is always being formed. Muktananda's initiation by Nityananda anticipates the whole of the journey. It brings together a guru's power to awaken the dormant spiritual energy of the seeker, a moment of intense love and tenderness, and an intrinsic understanding of the fundamental identity between God, Guru, and Self.

The separate themes crystallize only as portraits of our limited capacities. They reflect only the uneven readiness we bring to the task of realizing a truth that is indivisible, but which we grasp in partial ways. The three paths are all just approximations to the unitary path upon which all others converge in the end.

The ego and its residues are purified. An inner power wells up. The Other is established as the source of the power and as the Beloved. The relationship deepens, and with it the supreme paradox.

The Other is and is not. The Self blazes forth, forging the identity of Being between all forms of consciousness. It becomes a matter of choice whether one revels in that Oneness or delights in the apparent dualities. Every element of the synthesis is available to one who has reached the goal.

5 ▪ TRANSPERSONAL PSYCHOLOGY

What would be the content and form of a psychology capable of learning from the experiences and understandings presented in the Blue Pearl narrative? What are the implications of autobiographical accounts of spiritual evolution? What are the goals, methods, and assumptions that define the field of transpersonal psychology? These are the primary questions to which I turn in this final chapter.

Transpersonal psychology, as I see it, is defined by the primary place it gives to the concept of the absolute in its analysis of human life. This commitment to honoring the reality of the absolute should not be confused with a commitment to any specific imagery, formulation, or spiritual practice. Transpersonal psychology will perform a much needed function if it serves all the diverse systems of worship and scriptural narrative by providing each a place within its perimeter. If it can develop analytic categories that permit us to see the commonalities as well as the divergencies among the many ways of approaching the absolute, it will have greatly enriched the human community. Its task is not to amalgamate the systems of thought and practice that it explores but to create a common language for respectful inquiry and mutual appreciation.

Some people will choose to become or remain members, devotees, or practitioners of a specific spiritual tradition. Others will locate themselves only within the common ground created by transpersonal psychology: exploring, assessing the appeal of various teachings, or becoming more open to the many narratives of direct experience. Transpersonal psychology cannot achieve the internal consistency and powerful symbolism of any single spiritual path, but it can provide a series of bridges between superficially different accounts or world views. The challenge is to develop a conceptual scheme that, on the one hand, is informed by and open to an immense diversity of form and, on the other hand, yields an abstracted version of any specific tradition that the devotee would find to be a fair and acceptable version of his chosen path.

I propose to use the substance and implications of the Blue Pearl narrative to sketch out a version of transpersonal psychology. The place to start is with the absolute. Whereas scientific and clinical psychology deliberately and, it could be argued, wisely limit their concepts to what I label the relative domain, transpersonal psychology conceives of a reality that includes both relative and absolute. We shall see whether this two-category model of reality is transpersonal psychology's final word on the subject. For a start, however, there is no more essential assertion than that reality includes more than the temporary, conditional, causal universe.

This essay in the theory of transpersonal psychology begins with a review of some of the experiences and the intuitive formulations that lead human beings to include the absolute in their scheme of reality. We cannot proceed very far along this line before we must examine and question the way we think about the relative domain. It may be that the paradigm guiding our conception of physical and psychic reality is limiting our understanding of the role of the absolute in our daily lives. Only after reformulating our fundamental assumptions concerning observable reality can we develop a transpersonal psychology that appreciates both being and becoming, both the unchanging and the endless processes of transformation. Following this, we may explore transpersonal psychology's use of text in the service of self-awareness. Finally, we may extend the discussion of the absolute and the relative by considering how the domains of traditional and transpersonal psychology are related to one another. Perhaps the sense of duality and schism between these approaches to psychology can yield to a far more delicious intellectual outcome, the sense of paradox.

The Absolute as Image

The most unmistakable representations of the absolute are the personified characters in mythic and scriptural literature. We meet a god or goddess whose role is fundamentally different from any mortal also included in the story.

In the Blue Pearl narrative we enter a world that includes, among others, the Goddess Kundalinī, the indwelling Lord revealed as the Blue Person, and the primal source of all manifestation, the blue-throated Shiva. Muktananda's account of his spiritual journey proceeds with these focal characters either appearing in visual form or emerging as the inferred causes of numerous otherwise inexplicable developments. What this or any such account does is present us with *images of the absolute.*

When we are confronted by another person's system of images and stories, we are faced with some important choices. We can enter the symbolic, expressive world of the narrative and incorporate the images and symbols as part of our personal repertoire; we move thereby toward adopting a specific religion or spiritual path. We can make an internal translation of the image that permits us to resonate to the understanding that the imagery encodes. Or, finally, we can reject both the image and the understanding. Transpersonal psychology is primarily the result of the second of these three options. It is congruent neither with the world of the devotee who revels in the particular set of imagery and makes it his own nor with the parsimonious world of academic and clinical psychology in which such images of the absolute may not be invoked without violating the rules of the game. Transpersonal psychology attempts to appreciate the insightful expressiveness of any image of the absolute without thereby making normative the cast of characters created by a particular tradition or visionary leader.

In the case of Muktananda's narrative, our assignment is to see how well we have heard him tell his story. We can enjoy the imagery and then adopt it or not, as we see fit. In either case, we can extract from it the conception of reality that it conveyed to him and might also convey to us.

What I learn about the absolute from the Blue Pearl narrative is not one single understanding; it is a conglomerate of understandings that open up one aspect after another of the nature and function of the absolute. The three themes, or coherent subclasses of imagery, point to three distinguishably different systems of experiencing and discussing the absolute. The first revolves around issues of purification and power. The absolute, often personified as the Goddess Kundalinī, is seen as the continuous source of a process of individual purification that leads, if the individual cooperates, to liberation. Muktananda invokes the Goddess as his way of representing the power or energy behind all the spontaneous physical and visionary experiences that were leading him to an irreversible freedom from the past and the future. One implication is made clear in numerous ways: This transformation is not something that one can do for oneself. It requires the intelligence, the power, and the clarity of purpose that reside only in the absolute. They are inherent properties of the Goddess. This is the first image, and it is associated particularly with the path of power and purification.

The second image is found in the passages that deal with the Blue Person. The welling up of devotion, the experience of awe, and the response of surrender all convey an aspect of the absolute. Love is the very nature of the absolute. The absolute is thus the source and dispenser of grace. The devotee's response of love is but a flourishing in the devotee's heart of the unforced, unconditional absolute. All these images convey the life-sustaining, connection-making aspect of reality that is, in this view, an essential attribute of the absolute. A direct encounter with the personified absolute brings into form an awareness that the Other exists. In such moments, the Other, however imagined, *is* the absolute, so every feature, every word becomes a revelation of the nature and teaching of the divine.

The third set of imagery, then, whether it be the dazzling Light, the serene Shiva, or the vision of universes being created from the sacred Center, turns us to a third understanding of reality. It is an understanding of Being, of unity and equality, and it is personified in the form of Shiva. It is Shiva's state, primarily, and the state of the human teacher, Nityananda, that are suggested by the complex imagery. Through seeing the Blue Pearl in each person he met, Muktananda's awareness of the absolute expanded to the eventual climax of final realization. Distinctions between God, guru, and oneself, or between this person and another, were dissolved into the more fundamental perception of equality and identity. Central to this image stands the personified Shiva whose state entails a constant appreciation of the underlying unity of all things because he is aware of their common origin and essence which is Himself, his one pure Consciousness.

The Blue Pearl narrative thus presents us with three images of the absolute that convey their interpenetrating but distinct constructions of reality. How can we register them in the common understanding of transpersonal psychology without doing violence to their integrity?

There are those, including perhaps all of us at one point or another in our lives, who have become allergic to any mention of specific imagery, naming, or personification of the absolute. I need not catalog the reasons why such allergies develop. At issue is whether, in turning away from the forms contained in such imagery, we need thereby reject or exclude all mention of the absolute. In the Blue Pearl narrative, Muktananda shares one vivid image after another, but I doubt that he is trying thereby to increase our storehouse of visualizations. Rather, he is trying to affect our understanding, particularly our understanding of the absolute.

The Absolute as Principle

The task before us is to look beyond the image to the understandings which any narrative also contains. The spiritual autobiographies and scriptural accounts that transpersonal psychology may draw upon contain their own internal translations, linking the imagery with formulations of *the absolute as principle*.

The three sets of images presented in the three previous chapters convey a threefold formulation concerning the nature of the absolute as principle. In the first, the absolute is of the nature of freedom; all of existence is guided by a principle or power that moves it toward the state of ultimate freedom or liberation. The contrast is clear: the principle of liberation versus the principle behind ordinary life in which limitation and impurity, compounded by a lack of self-control, lead to a life of desire and pain. In the second, the absolute is of the nature of love. Love is God; God is love, manifesting as salvation, grace, guidance, and forgiveness. Love stands in contradistinction to the principle of ordinary life that manifests as pride, separateness, or unresponsiveness to life and joy. Finally, the third principle is awareness or consciousness, the basis of reality's oneness and sheer existence or Being. This intuition forms in contrast to the ordinary principle behind the sense of endlessly proliferating fragmentation, meaninglessness, and an eventual decay and death of all things.

Three principles are thus suggested throughout the Blue Pearl narrative: freedom, love, and consciousness. Each brings into words, with help from a particular scriptural and poetic tradition, the direct experiences that form the basis of Muktananda's teachings. The Upanishads, Kashmir Shaivism, and the Maharashtran poet-saints all lend a hand in giving form to his experiences and their implications. He translates the visions into understandings of the nature of the absolute, as do virtually all such texts. The absolute is something "experienced" as imagery and "known" as intuition. The image and the intuition are the means by which one is transformed and the fruit of one's prior spiritual development. Whether personified as the supreme actor in our human drama or inferred as a governing principle of the universe, representations of the absolute form a model of reality.

The fundamental assertion of any world view that includes the absolute is that reality can be divided, at least provisionally, for the purpose of analysis, into two orders: the relative and the absolute. In the world of the relative we find a symmetry of mutual interactions: Nothing influences something else without itself being altered, however slightly. In addition, we find or assume that each effect can be traced back to proximal and distal causes in a unbroken chain of cause and effect connections. In the world that contains both relative and absolute, however, we find asymmetries: Effects are attributed to absolute causes without implying that the absolute is thereby altered in any way. To construe the absolute as a cause is to construe a chain of causal connections that ends with the absolute. One need look no further, imagining that the absolute must also have its antecedent conditions. The absolute creates and continually modifies the realm of the relative, but remains itself unchanged, perfect. The implicit assumption that the relation between the absolute and the relative is asymmetrical is easiest to discern when the narrative includes a personified image of the absolute.

A god or a goddess is known by his or her ability to influence us mortals without being reciprocally influenced by us. Many of the words that have been applied to god-figures testify to this asymmetry: free, independent, self-born, unconditioned, pure, and untainted.

Let us briefly recall some of the ways the Blue Pearl narrative portrays the asymmetrical relationships between such images and the human seeker, Muktananda. The Goddess Kundalinī is in control of Muktananda's spiritual evolution. She knows the goal and the route thereto. His account leaves no doubt that her power and intelligence are totally independent of humanity. It is unthinkable to imagine the Goddess learning from or draining energy from any or all seekers. Whether they persist or quit, reach the liberated state or not, the Goddess remains the same. Imperviousness to reciprocal influence is one of the defining characteristics of an image of the absolute. It is similarly unthinkable to imagine that the love radiating from the Blue Person would wax or wane as a result of the devotion or rejection he might receive from Muktananda or any human figure in such a drama. Humans become discouraged when their love is not returned or upset when their beloved turns away, but god-figures do not, by definition. As well, the constantly blazing Light and the fully expanded Consciousness that are the very nature of the personified Shiva are not diminished by the presence, in the human realm, of darkness, ignorance, and forgetfulness.

The same issue of symmetry or asymmetry that we found in personified images of the absolute persists when we turn to the absolute as principle. In a world view that includes only the relative, love, freedom, or conscious awareness are treated as themselves derivatives of human growth and interactions. In a view that includes both absolute and relative, these same principles tend to be treated as prior, independent, and unaffected by any human event. From this perspective Truth is spoken of as something that exists, in its own order of reality, and functions as an active force that influences, asymmetrically, the course of human thought. Beauty is not treated as a descriptive attribute that humans create and apply, with shifting criteria, but as a preexistent source of inspiration that can neither be perfected nor spoiled by human effort. Love, as a principle, is understood to play upon the range of human interaction, but it can be neither forced nor depleted.

The Relative Domain

Before undertaking a fuller discussion of the absolute, we need to explore the world of the relative, particularly as defined by the field of psychology. Traditional academic psychology derives from the atomistic world view first developed by the Greek materialists, Democritus and others. In this view, what we can measure and compare—the observable universe—emerges from a substratum composed of small, primal elements or building blocks. In psychology's version of atomism the building block is the elemental habit or the firing of a neuron and its inhibition. From these primary elements and the primary relations among them psychology has tried to construct a model to explain the proliferated variety of human thought and action.

Newton's laws of thermodynamics are a masterful demonstration of the power and usefulness of this world view. Psychology's yearning for an equally powerful and useful perspective led it to behaviorism and the search for an elemental unit, be it habit or response. The search for a common explanatory system recurs throughout the range of the field's concerns. The complex is to be understood in terms of the simple. The lawful permutations and combinations of constituent parts create the emergent hierarchy of larger and larger wholes, and the occurrence of an intricate event may be traced back, or "reduced," to its component parts and their rudimentary interactions. The complex mental experience, for example, may be traced to muscular or neurochemical components. In all these ways, reductionism holds out the promise of explaining an event by tracing it back to lower and more primary causal factors.

How satisfactory is this reductionistic, deterministic approach to human events? As with Newtonian physics, one can see areas of enormous success, predictions confirmed and new research unfolding, but one can also detect limits beyond which the underlying paradigm breaks down. The empirical evidence of quantum physics marks the outer limit of the usefulness of Newtonian physics. The old order's analysis of the material world has not been overthrown, but it has been found to be limited. I suspect that when the limits of deterministic psychology are finally acknowledged, the data found to be beyond its capacity will turn out not to be new data at all but, rather, modern demonstrations of age-old capacities and potentials.

The phenomenon of remote viewing is but one small part of the data that will eventually force us to expand our fundamental perspectives.

There are important parallels between the implications of remote viewing for psychology and the impact of the evidence from quantum physics on the classical view of Newtonian physics. These parallels will be clearer if we review, briefly, some important developments in the field of theoretical physics.

As summarized by David Bohm, a quantum theorist with a strong interest in the development of models of reality, the situation is this. The classical view holds that matter is analyzable into elements that are entirely outside of each other and that influence each other only when they are contiguous; causality thus rests upon the principle of locality. Any demonstration, therefore, that shows events in one area to be correlated with events in an area "spacially separated" from the first presents us with data beyond the range of the classical view. Spacial separation between areas is defined by the impossibility of any known form of intercommunication between them, given the upper limit imposed by the speed of light. Precisely such a demonstration is found in the results of a hypothetical experiment proposed by Einstein, Podolsky, and Rosen, later reframed in a parallel form by Bohm, and recently found to be empirically grounded by the laboratory studies of Freedman and Clauser.[1] The problematic situation, as described by Bohm, is as follows:

> Consider a molecule of zero total spin, consisting of two atoms of spin, h/2. Let this molecule be disintegrated by a method not influencing the spin of either atom. The total spin then remains zero, even while the atoms are flying apart and have ceased to interact appreciably.
>
> Now, if any component of the spin of one of the atoms (say A) is measured, then because the total spin is zero, we can immediately conclude that this component of the spin of the other atom (B) is precisely opposite. Thus, by measuring any component of the spin of atom A, we can obtain this component of the spin of atom B, *without interacting with atom B in any way . . . .*

> . . . The problem is made even more difficult if we consider that, while the atoms are still in flight, we are free to reorientate the observing apparatus arbitrarily, and in this way to measure the spin of atom A in some other direction. This change is somehow transmitted *immediately* to atom B, which responds accordingly. Thus, we are led to contradict one of the basic principles of the theory of relativity, which states that no physical influences can be propagated faster than light.[2]

If we join Bohm in ruling out the possibility of a signal passing from atom A to atom B, we cannot comprehend their correlated states without turning to a radically different model of reality, a model positing not a fundamental level of separately analyzable elements but, rather, a fundamental "undivided wholeness," to use Bohm's term. Quantum theory's three major assertions all challenge the atomic, mechanistic model of reality: 1) movement is discontinuous; 2) the observed property of an entity (e.g., its registering as a wave or a particle) depends on the experimental situation in which it is observed; and 3) entities can be related to one another through non-local, non-causal connections. Each assertion helps to build the case that a model of reality wherein undivided wholeness is primary is consistent with data that cannot be understood within the classical Newtonian model. As Bohm puts it, " . . . the entire universe has to be thought of as an unbroken whole."[3]

What is needed is a model of reality that takes into account not only the obvious evidence of separateness provided by some experiences and some laboratory experiments but, as well, the unbroken wholeness revealed by other experiences and other laboratory evidence. Bohm names his version of such a model *the implicate order*.

Bohm's model, on the one hand, draws from and is directed toward the limited range of purely physical events. It is meant to stand or fall according to whether it makes sense of otherwise disorienting experimental evidence at that one level of observation. On the other hand, it is a model of reality that also provides ample room for speculation and further model-building. It is open to speculation about wholeness in the realm of human consciousness, and it is open to model-building that includes the absolute as a fundamental category of reality.[4]

In place of the fundamental, separately analyzable element, Bohm speaks of a fundamental wholeness. Within that wholeness, he distinguishes between the *explicate order,* which is the world of at least temporarily stable, observable matter or thought, and the *implicate order,* which is the vast ocean of unmanifest reality upon which the explicate rests, from which it emerges, and back to which it returns. The explicate is the gross and the implicate is the subtle version of the relative universe. Explicate is manifest; implicate is unmanifest. At least for the purpose of discussion, he proposes to make this distinction and explore how the unbroken wholeness of the implicate order emerges into or explicates as the world of discernable form and apparent separateness.

Bohm inverts the traditional atomistic assertion of what is primary; interconnectedness is taken as given. Unconnectedness and the sense of separateness are what need explanation, since it is they that are secondary and emergent phenomena. This stands in sharp contrast to the classical view in which the problem is how interdependence and mutuality can overcome the fragmentation that is presumed to be primary in nature. For Bohm's version of the Einstein-Podolsky-Rosen experiment the question "How can atom A possibly communicate with atom B?" loses its hold on us and is replaced by such questions as "How does the one underlying implicate order of reality manifest, in the explicate order, as two atoms, A and B, whose spin remains correlated even though they are flying apart from each other?" Bohm's model of reality moves even closer to home for me, however, if I turn from the two atoms, A and B, to the remote viewing pair, the subject and the outbound experimenter introduced in the second chapter.

If we ask how the outbound experimenter's experience of the playing field or the bowling alley can possibly affect the subject as he sits in the basement lab, it matters greatly what we are assuming when we ask our question. Are we assuming that the pair of people involved are ultimately separate from one another or ultimately manifestations of a larger whole, a deeper reality? The assumption of separateness makes remote viewing seem impossible. The interconnectedness that is revealed in such phenomena seems too far removed from the natural human condition of mutual isolation. In contrast, to invoke the implicate order model is to assume that it is dividing lines that are ephemeral, and separation is the state that needs to be constantly reestablished by maintaining barriers and boundaries.

The implicate order and the explicate order are mutually defining. The atom or the thought that emerges from the implicate order is but the "unfolding" of the then current totality of all matter or all thought. The explicate order is a "manifestation" of that larger order of reality, and when it, in its turn, destabilizes and is enfolded back into the unmanifest, implicate state, the implicate is thereby altered. It is, in Bohm's view, all one system in interaction. The implicate and the explicate are mutually interpenetrating aspects of the relative domain, and, therefore, it would be inappropriate to suggest that the implicate order plays the role of the absolute as discussed earlier in this chapter. The implicate order is not God by some other name, or even the realm of Platonic ideals. It is the residue and source of manifest reality. Its properties afford a much needed expansion of the ways we think about the world of matter and consciousness, but it is not a euphemism for the divine, the sacred, or the Other.

Bohm does allow for the possibility of an interplay between an "active intelligence" and the relative world of thought and matter. The role he assigns to "insight" as an active process beyond thought is left necessarily imprecise, but its effects are precisely those I attribute to the absolute as principle. I return to the conjunction of the relative and the absolute, but, for now, our questions center on the relative domain and how best to understand events at that level.[5]

How I "knew" that the outbound experimenter was in a bowling alley can be more comfortably discussed from the perspective of the implicate order, for the same reason that we can more comfortably discuss how atom B "knew" that atom A had had its spin changed. The unbounded wholeness is fully represented in each of the apparently separate entities into which it manifests, and each part is affected by every other part of the whole. Bohm, Pribram, and others have drawn analogies between this implicate order model and holographic photography.[6] In this lensless procedure the representation of the larger whole in each piece produced by slicing the film into separate parts seems a shocking violation of what common sense and the paradigm of classical physics lead us to expect. The implication of this analogy for remote viewing would be that the presence of veridical information in the subject's consciousness depends not on communication between the outbound experimenter and the subject but on having the subject gain access to the undivided wholeness of human consciousness already present within his apparently separate state. Since that wholeness contains—in an implicate form, Bohm might add—the registered experience of the outbound experimenter, the question becomes, "Under what conditions will the subject be open to that wholeness?" or "How or when does the implicate order unfold into a specific instance of remote viewing?"

How shall we think about the interplay of the implicate and the explicate order? How can we form a useful set of images to help us recall and apply the central assertions of this model of reality? Bohm has tried several ways of representing his model, and each one adds to our understanding. He likens the implicate to a flowing stream within which forms, for a while, a discernible whirlpool, here likened to an event in the explicate order. The whirlpool is not independent of the stream. They are as one, but the relatively stable pattern of the whirlpool makes it stand out as figure against the ground of the larger whole. Soon, however, the whirlpool loses its coherence and fades back into the undivided flow of the current.

Some of the model's assertions are more clearly captured in his image of the ocean. Bohm refers to the explicate as a wave that forms, temporarily, on the surface of the ocean's vast depths, and elsewhere he uses the analogy of the ocean in other ways that are particularly helpful. I will modify some of these images in order to capture some important characteristics of the model.

Imagine that the act of allowing a thought to register in our awareness is like the act of dipping a ladle into the ocean of all consciousness. The specific content of one moment's thought (an event in the explicate order) is thus derived from sampling the then current residue of the history of all human thought (the implicate order). Before long, this thought, as well, will dissolve and enter, as the effluent of this one moment, the thus altered ocean which will be sampled again in the next moment. If we see ourselves as the solitary crew in a vast flotilla of identical vessels, it is obvious that, in sampling the ocean on which we ride, we usually dip our ladle very close to the side of the ship. In general, the best predictor of what we will think one moment is what we were thinking just one moment before. There is a powerful redundancy, sometimes very useful and sometimes very discouraging, to the thought content of adjacent moments.

Psychology's study of the lawful relations between past and present or between individuals and their human context is, in this analogy, the study of where we dip our ladle other than right by the side of the boat. Sometimes we retrieve and declare ourselves affected by such ancient effluents as childhood memories or old grudges. Sometimes the ladle seems to be on the end of a short pole, sometimes one that is very long. At times, we retrieve and discover we are affected by the effluent of other members of our flotilla. In some of these instances we seem to have reached out to have our neighbor fill our ladle; the communication is direct and intended. However, this does not exhaust the possibilities.

The transfer into our consciousness of content that can be traced to our flotilla-mates' effluent may not be subject to observation. It may result from nonordinary retrievals of information, not through manifest communication but through the medium of the undivided ocean of human consciousness to which we have total access. We are, in this view, capable of being influenced by events in remote places and times, events beyond the possibility of any contiguous or local connection to our current situation, simply because all such events inevitably enter the wholeness of which our awareness is but a sample. The so-called psychic powers revealed in remote viewing are testimony to the unbroken wholeness, the ocean of consciousness, and not merely to the unique mental capacity of a successful subject.

The Relative and the Absolute

Bohm's paradigm of the implicate and explicate order offers us something far more important than one possible explanation for events in the relative domain. His model provides an opening for radically new ways to think about the role of the absolute.

When I recall the years just before I stopped entertaining any notion of the absolute whatever, I can easily spot the difficulty I was having with the concept. I couldn't think of a single plausible way that the absolute, which I then called God, could have any effect on the world. The idea of God helping push footballs over goal lines or win wars for our side had run its course and become untenable. My next image, of a powerful but utterly remote God, seemed irrelevant to any physical or mental event in the everyday world. At most, the category "God" provided a convenient bin in which to store my current conception of the highest qualities toward which human life might aspire. The absolute, as image, faded away, and the absolute as principle seemed an unnecessary gloss on the discussion of human values.

Now, as I review the personal experiences and trusted texts that have reopened the category of the absolute, I need above all to be clear how I would bring together the absolute and the relative as the dual aspects of reality. When Bohm proposes a paradigm shift that views the relative domain in terms of implicate and explicate orders, his model suggests a satisfying way to see how, at least potentially, the relative is capable of being modified by the existence of the absolute.

Bohm follows a slightly different route than I would follow. He refers to what I call the absolute as principle when he discusses insight and active intelligence. More recently, he has proposed seeing the implicate order, the wholeness of thought and matter, as itself ordered by a "super-implicate." This concept leads him to conclusions I would also endorse, but I find it comfortable to start my exploration by thinking about the absolute as image.[7]

Two images of the absolute recur in the Blue Pearl narrative. Taken together, they form a powerful model for considering the role of the absolute in the world of relative events. One suggests the ground of all existence, pure consciousness, the unmoving and the eternal. It is the image of unmanifest Being, the Sphere of unmanifest Light. It is Shiva. But this image is never far removed from images of the absolute as an active force, the source of all blessings, transformation, and grace. Shakti, the Goddess, appears throughout Muktananda's account as the agent behind one amazing, growth-producing event after another.

We could preserve these images, or we could see them in their equivalent form, as principles. Every attribute of the absolute as image, every registry of the nature of the absolute as form, is, in effect, a proposal for what some of those absolute principles might be. Accounts that personify the absolute as god-figure and explore how such a figure affects human beings through its actions and teachings capture the variety of insights into the workings of reality beyond those commonly thought to be merely natural processes of cause and effect. As Bohm points out, " . . . people had insight in the past about a form of intelligence that organized the universe and they personalized it and called it God. A similar insight can prevail today without personalizing it and without calling it a personal God."[8] Whether he or any of us prefers to personalize the principles is a matter of choice. The fact remains that we may use any account, whether personalized or not, as we attempt to list the properties of the absolute.

The Absolute as Tendency

Through image and principle, we are constantly struggling to capture an implication of our experience that, if unnamed, seems to slip through the filters of our awareness. All our words and stories, and even direct experiences, represent our effort to preserve the awesome inference that there is more than the relative order of reality.

What might be some of the absolute principles revealed by the process of our evolving lives? Our assignment is to discern *the absolute as tendency*. If we restrict ourselves to the realm of human consciousness, we may see that we attribute to the absolute three quite different processes: 1) the tendency to transform the contents of our consciousness so as to remove all sense of limitation and to maximize fearlessness, transcendence of desire, and attainment of liberation; 2) the tendency to overcome the imagined obstacles that divide us from each other and block the natural state of love; and 3) the tendency to alter our awareness so that we realize the unity of all things and recognize our inherent nature as, for example, pure consciousness.

We can notice the tendencies in operation only by noting a change in our state or in the state of someone whose evolution we can observe. Whether we do so through the image of the Goddess, Shakti, or through the principle or tendency underlying human transformation, we can record our sense of the asymmetrical operation of the absolute upon the relative. Something or some entity, as it were, seems to be guiding us, propelling us in magnificent directions. But how? At what point does this "intervention" occur?

I must return to the model of the implicate and explicate order to fashion my answer. The absolute, I would propose, is "built in" to the endless series of explications by which the unmanifest wholeness takes form. Just as the laws of thermodynamics refer to one set of tendencies, the absolute refers to a quite different set of tendencies reflected in the process of explication.

What we may call the absolute is not the only tendency in the system. Visions, miracles, ecstatic moments, and profound understandings happen to some people more than others and more at some times than at others. As with the case of remote viewing, the question of why such things happen can be paired with the question of why they do not.

The implicate order is the unmanifest wholeness of all thought, but, somehow, from that totality we retrieve, or are handed, a particular thought. On what basis? Why this thought and not that, or any other?

One basis suggests the operation of constancies. We see "the same thing," even if our angle changes or someone actually substitutes something slightly different in its place. Constancies are one sort of tendency affecting explication. Another basis determining what manifests suggests a gradual decay into randomness. We can't remember whole stanzas of our college anthem the way we once could. Some entropic process seems to disorder our efforts to recall past events. But there is another basis, another lawful process that operates and is noticed, sometimes. It is the process reflected in movement from one moment to another, or from one decade to another, movement toward greater freedom, love, and understanding.

Some people attribute these changes to "natural causes." Some feel they have been blessed. Important as these *post hoc* explanations are, what matters more is the change itself. A quantum jump from one level of freedom to another, one level of love to another, one experience of beauty or understanding to another—these shifts are the primary data of transpersonal psychology. Whether the shift is apparent in the flash of a moment's revelation or is incremental and seen only as a life project, what matters is the shift itself.

Each such confirmation of the existence and role of the absolute permits us to speculate further and more firmly about how it could be that reality tends inherently to further these tendencies toward freedom, love, and consciousness. To take but one example, what I learned from the experience of being a subject in the remote viewing experiment was that I am not as limited by space and time as I once thought. I am far more interconnected with people than I had imagined. To take the major case presented in this exploration, what Muktananda's experiences of the Blue Pearl showed him was the transforming power leading him to liberation, to the love that comes from the Other and yet is his own Self, and to his full identity with the very principle of Consciousness.

My inference that the absolute plays on the explicating form of our inner awareness is but one way to translate the experiences and understandings revealed in the Blue Pearl narrative. The source of the tendency toward liberation, love, and self-realization can be located, as Muktananda does, in the personified images of the absolute, but his purpose in recording his spiritual experiences would not be thwarted by proposing, more impersonally, that these tendencies are at work constantly in the undivided wholeness that manifests as our every thought and action. These tendencies are the very nature of the absolute.[9]

The Turn toward the Absolute

If our thoughts and actions of any given moment are the resultant of two sets of tendencies, which we may call the absolute and the relative, an important question that arises is, "How can we increase the role of the absolute in our lives?" In asking the question we may have in mind one or another aspect of the absolute. We may be wondering, for example, how we can accelerate the process of inner purification in order to gain power and freedom, including that freedom from the weight of the past and the allure of the future that is called liberation. We may be wondering how we can be more receptive to the tendency we call love, in whatever form or aspect. Or we may be wondering how the peace of mind that comes from directly experiencing the unity and equality of all being can replace the distracted, fragmented thinking we usually encounter within our awareness. We may be wondering, in effect, whether there is anything we can do to influence, or least not to impede, the tendencies of freedom, love, and consciousness that we wish were more evident in our lives.

Muktananda's narrative documents one way to intensify the role of the absolute. He approached and accepted Nityananda as his guru, and the end of his searching was to recognize the absolute as his Self. His final realization of the identity between God, Guru, and Self can be expanded into three statements. Gods exists. The Guru is God. I am God. These three statements can be examined in the context of this discussion of the absolute as tendency.

That "God exists" can be known if one senses the tendency toward freedom, love, and enlightenment playing in one's life. The statement locates the source of the transformative tendency as the absolute. That "The Guru is God" can be known if one experiences the operation of that tendency especially when one is in the presence of the guru, thinking of him, or carrying out his suggestions. The identity of God and Guru is inferred by Muktananda because no useful boundary could be preserved between the effect of the Goddess and the effect of the guru. Their impact was identical; hence the conclusion that the Goddess was taking the form of Nityananda. That "I am God" merely continues the erosion of illusory boundaries. The transforming tendency is located "within." The Center as sacred source, experienced as the Self, is no less the agent of the transforming events. Turning within is the same as being in the guru's presence. The climactic vision merges all three images—Shiva, Nityananda, and Muktananda. These names and forms become interchangeable representations of the same inherent tendency of all reality, the tendency toward the ultimate realization.

The image of the active Goddess represents the tendency toward the goal. The image of Shiva represents the goal. The goal and the path to the goal are inseparably joined into one complex unity. The goal is reached when one enters the state of Shiva. At that point, the paradoxes enunciated by the Blue Person take hold. It is a state of being here and everywhere. It is a state of perfect stillness and, no less, spontaneous and appropriate action. The tendencies by which the Goddess alters the manifest content of thought and action are also at play in the guru, as both a source of his own delight and a source of the transformation of those who come in contact with him. For Muktananda, his guru, Nityananda, was the manifestation in form of Shiva and of Shakti, the goal and the means.

One way to think further about this question is to return to the distinction between ego and Self. Some people think about the Self as if they had in mind an image of the absolute, while others consider it as if it were a principle. The two modes are not fundamentally different, and it is common to find that one shifts back and forth between the two ways of talking about the Self. However, when it comes to wondering what one can do to change one's life, it matters how one conceives of the Self. For those who see the Self in image form, as what might even seem to be an inner Other, the goals of the spiritual quest involve "getting in touch with the Self" or "letting the Self take over." The image is of an inner entity we are having a hard time contacting, and this, in turn, raises questions about what layers of non-Self may be obscuring easy contact or what "noise in the system" is garbling the signal from the inner Self. However, all constructions of the Self as image have their counterpart in the alternative way of talking about the Self, as principle.

The Self as principle can be understood both in terms of the goal and the process that moves us toward the goal. We can think about the goal states of freedom, love, or pure consciousness as the nature of the Self, but we can also see all the forces that move us toward those goals as the absolute tendencies of the Self that move in the universe. The question becomes: "What impedes or weakens the operation of these tendencies?"

The Self as tendency can be seen in relation to the other class of tendencies organized under the label of "ego." The ego is the source of all the tendencies that derive from the sense of separateness and our preoccupation with gain or loss or with satiation or pain, as experienced by the isolated individual we construe ourselves to be. The ego is the inferred tendency behind our preoccupation with "I and mine." However, it is a matter of choice whether we consider the ego as principle or imagine, instead, a devious internal character named "The Ego" who plays an obstructive role in the drama of our spiritual development. It is not mere carelessness of thinking that leads us, at times, to fashion such elaborate constructions as "The ego wouldn't let go" or "The ego is our worst enemy." The fact that we speak in such dramatic language is evidence of how vividly we experience the operation of egoic tendencies within our thinking and action.

Meditation and the Teacher

However we conceive of them, the question remains, "How can the balance between ego and Self be altered in the direction of the Self?" Every spiritual tradition organizes its answers to this question by providing a set of methods or techniques for the seeker. Each tradition suggests the kinds of austerities, practices, prayers, uplifting stories, and forms of contemplation that have worked and will, hopefully, work again to maximize the tendencies of the Self. The Blue Pearl narrative points us toward two methods for courting the transformative process. Muktananda's experiences and teachings flow directly from the practice of meditation under the guidance of an accomplished teacher.

"What is meditation?" and "What is the role of the teacher?" are the two questions we may explore next. In doing so, we need to be aware of the commonalities that exist between Muktananda's approach to the Self and the wide range of apparently dissimilar methods used by other spiritual traditions.

Meditation is designed to help us move beyond the confines of the ego and move toward realizing the Self. It is also a technique for altering our usual way of retrieving memory and information from the implicate order, the ocean of human consciousness. These two descriptions of the purpose and consequences of meditation are not identical, however. The former suggests an infusion of the absolute into our consciousness; the latter suggests merely a nonordinary perception of the contents of the relative domain in all its wholeness. It may be useful to explore some of the implications of this latter effect of meditation. Meditation entails a gradual stilling of the mind's internal chatter and buzz. Under these conditions, we may retrieve many old memories; we may even experience directly the thoughts and perceptions of other people, as in remote viewing.

The evidence suggests that those who have meditated for years or who have just finished a period of meditation succeed better at remote viewing and similar tasks than those who have never meditated. In the short run, the practice of meditation seems to allow us to expand our boundary, partly through stilling recursive private thoughts and sensory input. In the long run, some may use the practice as part of a genuine movement toward the Self, while others will only have their ego strengthened by becoming pridefully attached to their great powers.

Spiritual teachers regularly warn against the temptation of confusing psychic powers with the working of the absolute. As Muktananda put it to a group of researchers, "These petty miracles are very ordinary." He then went on to suggest that remote viewing was inherently no more wonderful than any perceptual ability; in fact, it tempts one, as does all outward turning of one's consciousness, to neglect the goal of realizing the Self.[10] Without an understanding of the nature of Self, the ego can become more rather than less entrenched following the experience of remote viewing. If this is so, then it follows that it is not the phenomenon of remote viewing, per se, that shows the operation of the absolute but, rather, the altered understanding of reality sometimes produced by such experiences. The warnings of the spiritual teachers are all the more urgent because the move toward liberation, which entails a radical revision of one's self-image in the direction of freedom, may result in having all the so-called psychic powers come to one "unbidden." The task of accepting such increases in "personal power" without thereby jeopardizing the understandings that lead to liberation is a notoriously difficult one.

The technique of meditation is a spiritual practice which is designed to loosen the hold of the egoic patterns that determine how we describe ourselves and how we view others. It does this by generating the optimum conditions for the mind to register something beyond its usual tendencies and assumptions. Reduce the input of sensory data, invoke the Other's presence and guidance, affirm through a mantra or some other device one's inner nature as divine, witness nonjudgmentally the ensuing flow of consciousness, and what then transpires may be the representation of all the tendencies that lead beyond the ego. The body seems to be moved, purified; the imagery has an unfamilar and awesome clarity; the spontaneous registry of what one's life and current experiences all imply at their core may take the form of searing insights. Even the stillness comes as a blessing and a discovery. Whatever happens, it continues to suggest a shift in the inner structure of one's consciousness, a shift from ego to Self.

There are, however, many pitfalls to this process of meditation. The Blue Pearl narrative documents one pitfall most poignantly. Muktananda had fallen into the trap of pride, the trap of prematurely considering that his yogic attainments signaled the completion of his spiritual journey. Therefore, his narrative attests the twofold nature of the method that succeeded for him: meditation *and* the guidance of the teacher. It is the teacher and the corrective power of scripture that operate in tandem with meditation, each complementing the other, counter-balancing experience and guidance. Muktananda's teacher sent him back to his meditation hut, and the process continued. Direct guidance is only one aspect of the teacher's role. Beyond the puncturing of inflated conclusions about one's attainment, beyond specifying appropriate techniques, and beyond the confirmation of significant, even ultimate, progress, the teacher-disciple bond, as revealed throughout the Blue Pearl narrative, entails the most profound of human connections.

Muktananda's experiences convinced him that he was receiving the contents of his meditative experience directly from the accumulated awareness and imagery of his accomplished teacher. The bond that unites teacher and disciple goes beyond manifest, observable communication. Not all traditions construe the teacher's role in this way, just as they may not employ meditation as a formal practice, but the Blue Pearl narrative suggests that the living teacher may be seen as the personification of the absolute. The teacher is the source of the transforming tendencies that lead the seeker toward freedom, love, and consciousness. The teacher represents and leads the disciple toward the Self. Muktananda's explanation of the transformative experiences he presents in the narrative is never far from the assertion that his teacher was "doing everything." From the day of his initiation to the climax of self-realization, the teacher "gives" Muktananda the imagery, the awareness, the fearlessness, and whatever else it takes to accomplish full realization of the Self. However, these asymmetrical images of receiving from the Other are permitted to coexist with the superficially contradictory awareness that there is no Other, that the teacher and disciple are one.

The visual imagery of Muktananda's final realization preserves not only the devotee's stance of surrender and gratitude but the realized being's stance of full equality with the absolute, as represented through the forms of his teacher and Lord Shiva and through the formless reality of pure Consciousness. His teacher gave him that state, but it was no less true that the state was, and always had been, his own nature that he could now, finally, recognize and affirm.

One implication of this understanding of the role of the teacher is that the teacher cannot teach what he has not attained. The balance between ego and Self in the teacher sets a probable limit for the disciple's transformation. This is made all the more plausible if we realize that the process of teaching takes place not only at the level of guidance and verbal communication but by direct transmission.

The closer the bond between the seeker and teacher, the more the seeker's meditation will entail receiving directly what the teacher has to teach. Physical separation is not an insurmountable barrier, nor, if we take seriously the evidence from the world's great religions, does the teacher need to be alive or be, as some would put it, "in his body." If the implicate order contains all the enfolded residue of the past, then it is theoretically possible to retrieve the presence, the teaching, and the state of a teacher from any age or culture. The focal point of one's meditation may thus range from a specific teacher to the history of one's people to the nearly universal archetypes that move us toward freedom, love, and pure consciousness. The images or the events that we recall are not, in and of themselves, the sacred, but they play a crucial role in the transformative process that reveals the absolute in our lives. The Blue Pearl is one recorded image of the absolute, and it is worth recalling the many ways that Muktananda used this vision to move toward realization of the Self. The sum total of all his meditative experiences led him "beyond the Blue Pearl," to an intuition of the formless absolute, but this in no way negates the fact that the image was a perfect vehicle for his evolving spiritual development.

The Practice of Transpersonal Psychology

The Blue Pearl narrative reveals the effects of two techniques available to anyone exploring transpersonal psychology—meditation and the guidance of a spiritual teacher. It also contains many examples of the practice I have employed in the present project: working with text. The list of potential practices is very long, but their goal always includes our own transformation. Transpersonal psychology requires us to examine ourselves and acknowledge our yearning, our attainment, and the impediments to further growth. We are the primary case of our own research. The purpose of an ongoing practice is to manifest those tendencies that we may call the Self and to diminish the strength of those we may call the ego.

How then does one become an effective transpersonal psychologist? What does it take to recognize and learn from the data offered us by the human record of seeking, attaining, backsliding from, rediscovering, and irreversibly realizing the absolute? My conclusion is that we can only learn from others to the extent that we are learning for ourselves. Our direct experience and our understanding must be expanding if we hope to make full use of the data offered us by others.

Only in transpersonal psychology do we encounter so inescapably the idea that we could, even should, learn about the author of our chosen text by becoming, in our unique way, as much like that person as possible. Scientists have followed a different strategy and have constructed apparatus or trained observers to be objective, to yield the same results as the adjacent apparatus or observer. Their strategy fits well their goal of determining the lawful relations among observed objects. Transpersonal psychology, however, needs a different strategy since it aims at a different conclusion altogether.

I have come to understand the goal of transpersonal psychology as the bringing together of the diverse human techniques, experiences, and understandings in order that any person, including especially the transpersonal psychologist, may realize the role of the absolute in human life. This task forces us to take stock of what we know on the basis of our direct experience. We cannot be increasingly open to scriptural and autobiographical accounts unless we have an ongoing practice and a growing set of self-evident understandings. Our capacity for empathic and accurate accounts of what others are saying depends on the depth, complexity, and availability of our own inner understandings. How do these understandings develop?

Many of the things that psychologists already do are directed to the goals of deepening experience, sifting its subtle meanings, and enhancing personal growth. The purposes, even if unacknowledged, of therapy often include the goal of knowing the ultimate layer of self. Psychologists not only recommend but also employ on themselves the valuable techniques of dream analysis, keeping a careful diary, and various forms of meditation. Efforts at self-development and efforts to become a more effective researcher in the realm of transpersonal psychology cannot be easily divided from each other; each augments the other. The goal of transpersonal psychology is both private and collective. We can only learn these things one by one, in our own way and our own good time, but, still, we can be helpful by encouraging each other, sharing our progress reports, and building a common language for communication.

The question of how we can assess the progress we are making toward understanding the absolute leads in several directions. One line of inquiry starts with our experience, another with the way we frame our understandings, and a third with how we live our lives as an expression of what we understand.

Direct evidence, especially when tested and validated by one's teacher or scriptural reference points, is the most useful indication of the transformative process. We can use our power, our joy, and our sense of unity with all being to measure our appreciation of the absolute. The distance between our lives and the lives of those in whom the absolute as principle is fully flowering can be narrowed. However, transpersonal psychology is concerned with more than the experience of freedom, love, and awareness; it is concerned, as well, with what we do to block these states, since how we view ourselves has a great impact upon our maturing understanding of the absolute.

A sharpened sense of how the ego operates is as much a part of spiritual development as the growing perception of the absolute. As we come to know how pervasive, how subtle, and how powerful are the effects of the egoic assumption system, we can become more conscious of the choices we are making and more able to recognize the play of the many tendencies within us. As this insight develops, so too does the capacity to form and sustain the self-understanding that facilitates the workings of the Self.

The interplay of experience and understanding is what sustains the process of transformation. More than any single experience or formulation, what impresses me about the life story of those who have reached the goal of realizing the Self is their capacity to construct and preserve complex, paradoxical systems of understandings. The Blue Pearl narrative shows how easily Muktananda moves among events and verbal statements that would impel most of us to resist the implicit paradoxes and ask, "Which is it?" Does the divine exist in form or is the formless absolute the only reality? Did God create us or did we create God? Is there an Other or only the one Self?

We ask all these questions because we have not had the experiences necessary to embrace both alternatives at once. Our experiences will not sustain answers of such paradoxical complexity as "Yes, both are true." I can only surmise how it might feel to attain such a state, but it appears that the ability to encompass, simultaneously, both or all parts of a paradoxical understanding is built on a wealth of experience. One essential part of Muktananda's experience was that visions which one might imagine would jar against one another did not in fact do so. Muktananda remained unswervingly loyal to the validity of his experience. To break the paradox and settle for only one component of his understanding would be to disaffirm the wholeness of his meditative visions, and that he would not do. There were moments of encountering the Other and moments of realizing that the Other and he were but various guises of the one Self. The paradox is sustained by the diversity of his direct experience.

One way to pursue the issue of paradox is to scan our conceptual system for the either/or's that seem a bit too well established. Distinctions that are maintained with a special fervor or defensiveness sometimes indicate an unnecessary polarization. One such distinction just may be the absolute vs. the relative.

We create the split when we slide from saying that the spontaneous tendency toward freedom, love, and understanding suggests the absolute to saying that the absolute is defined by only such marvelous tendencies. Similarly, when we slide from acknowledging the absolute in the form of the inner Self to excluding the ego from the realm of the absolute, we may go on to despise the very existence of the ego. The temptation to move from asserting the existence of the absolute to limiting it only to that which is good and lovely inverts our initial predicament. Where before we were enjoined to deny or ignore the absolute, we are soon urging ourselves and others to ignore or disparage the relative. Nothing could be farther from the teachings of the Blue Pearl narrative.

From the perspective of one who can fully recognize the absolute, the so-called relative is just another form that the absolute may take. Some tendencies lead us toward remembrance of our essential Self, and some do not. But even these latter are the workings of the absolute. They deserve another label by which to mark their function. If we prefer to think of the absolute as image, we may dwell, as did St. John of the Cross, on the divine intention that gives rise to even "the dark night of the soul," the intense suffering of ego death preceding liberation. For what purpose do these torments occur? As a test, as a purification, and as a teaching. If, on the other hand, we prefer to think of the absolute as principle, we may conclude, as Kashmir Shaivism does, that the absolute functions not only through grace but through concealment. The universe, in this view, is a play of both concealment *and* revelation or grace. There is creation, but there is also destruction. There is illumination but also ignorance.

The teacher's categories, "absolute" and "relative," were meant to awaken us and expand our narrow vision, but once grasped they are shown to be serving the teacher's larger task of conveying a radical but paradoxical vision of reality. Our initial model of reality that excluded the absolute can yield to a second, dichotomous model that encompasses both absolute and relative. This second model, in its turn, can yield to a third model that distinguishes between motion toward and motion away from the light but concludes that all motion reveals equally the one process of evolution toward self-realization.

At one stage in our development, we need to be introduced to the reality of the absolute that shines through the illusory appearances in which we have become enmeshed. But then there comes a time when the distinction between absolute and relative needs to be dissolved into a nondualistic understanding that there is only one reality, whether it be called God, Consciousness, the Tao, or Being.

The tension of paradox grows when, as these models shift back and forth in my mind, I find myself entertaining two deeply held convictions that I can neither reconcile nor negate. There are miles to go. There is nothing to do.

We can sense that there is no separation between the absolute and the relative without losing the additional sense of being on a long journey. It is thus that I come to wonder how this vehicle—this psyche of mine—came to have the strengths and weaknesses that it has. The findings of traditional psychology are certainly relevant to any effort to understand why the journey can often be so difficult.

Transpersonal psychology's role is to enlarge how we study and think about human life, not to eliminate the old concerns from psychology's agenda. Looked at in the light of a larger synthesis of transpersonal and traditional psychology, much of what has already been done in traditional psychology provides essential information on how the ego develops, works, and thwarts its own transcendence. Psychology's documentation of human functioning yields an important but partial portrait of the full range of our possible development. Few of our pathetically self-serving and small-minded inclinations have gone unnoticed. Psychology's assessment may not grasp all that we are, but it is often valid as far as it goes. We can only gain from seeing that, Yes, we do think like this, harbor these drives, seek these advantages, and resist our further growth in many ways. A psychology that can integrate consideration of the negative and positive features will be in the strongest possible position to understand our lives, and there is no need to locate transpersonal psychology in an either/or relation to all that psychology has contained over the past hundred years.

From one, final perspective, what matters is neither experience nor understanding, but how these, together, transform our lives and relations with the rest of the world. In the case of Swami Muktananda, his meditative visions and his understanding of the absolute in the form of the Goddess Kundalinī sustained not only the process of his purification but also his attainment of the state of liberation. This in turn led to his power to guide and validate the same purificatory process in others. He became a teacher capable of awakening an awareness of the absolute within a person and then guiding the person to the final goal. His visions of the personified, indwelling Lord led directly to the fact that he was able to teach, by his example, how to welcome others with love and respect. He was truly available, in a spirit of total acceptance, because he saw and was therefore impelled to worship each person as a direct manifestation of the divine. Finally, as a result of his visionary experience of his and everyone's identity with the divine, he was able to impart his state of unity awareness to others, through their vision of the Blue Pearl or through their sense of a fundamental oneness.

To the extent that our experiences and understandings are teaching us about the absolute, we can expect profound changes in how we relate to ourselves and to others. We can expect profound changes, as well, in the effectiveness and certainty with which we utilize our capacities in the everyday world. The promise entails more than hearing about someone else's freedom or capacity for love. The promise is that, in one way or another, we will see our lives change. If studying the lives of remarkable beings and struggling to understand the implications of their experiences and teachings can contribute to this transformation of lives, then transpersonal psychology has an honorable role to play in human development.

GLOSSARY

āp in Hindi, the second person pronoun, used to express respect or deference, as distinct from *tum* and *tū* used in more familiar contexts

abhanga a metrical form used in the devotional poetry of many Maharashtran poet-saints

Advaita (lit. not two) a nondualistic school of monistic idealism, such as Vedānta, which infers from direct experience the one eternal Self, the Witness of all knowledge

ahamkāra (*ahaṁkāra*) the ego, one aspect of the four-fold psychic instrument described by Patanjali, is defined by the tendency to create a bounded sense of "me" and "mine" and to view everything from that egoic point of reference

Airavata (*Airāvata*) an elephant in the heaven-world of Indra

ājnā (*ājñā*) (lit. order, command) the *ājnā chakra* refers to the plexus of subtle connections associated physically with the area between the eyebrows and understood experientially as the inner seat of "the other" (*itara*), in the form of Paramashiva or the primal Guru

ākāsha (*ākāśa*) the subtle inner space or ether

Arjuna the human figure whose dialogue with Krishna in the *Bhagavad Gita* presents a series of teachings on selfless action, duty, devotion, and the supreme nondual reality *āsana* a yogic posture designed to increase the body's capacity for natural stability and balance

āshram (*āśrama*) a setting for spiritual practices, usually under the direction of a teacher or master of *yoga*

ātman the Self, absolute reality, pure being

Aum the three component letters of the mystical syllable, *OM*, the primal sound as described in the Mandukya Upanishad

Baba (lit. Father) a term of affection and respect for a father, a relative, or a holy man

Bhagavān the Lord, giver of blessings; also, a traditional term of honor for a holy person

Bhagavad-Gītā the dialogue between Krishna and Arjuna which was incorporated into the text of the epic *Mahabharata* toward the end of the pre-Christian era

bhakti the practice and experience of devotion; hence *bhakta*, one whose spiritual orientation is primarily devotional

Bhavānī the supreme conscious creative power, depicted as the Goddess in the *Vijnanabhairava bindu* (lit. drop) the primal form, a compacted sphere of all potential, emerging into actuality, sometimes experienced via an intense visual representation, e.g., the Blue Pearl

Brahmā the power and tendency to create, sometimes personified, together with Vishnu and Shiva, as part of the Hindu trinity

Brahman supreme reality, sometimes identified, as in the Upanishadic texts, with the threefold experience of existence, consciousness, and bliss; hence, the compound name for *Brahman*: *Satchidananda brahmarandhra* (lit. the hole of Brahman) the topmost spiritual center, a localization of pure consciousness at or just above the top of the head, also known as the *sahasrara*

buddhi the intellect, one of the fourfold aspects of the psychic instrument described by Patanjali, whereby the individual consciousness reflects the light of the absolute, or the Self, and is able to discriminate between what is real and what is illusion

chakra (*cakra*) one of a system of latent or potential subtle energies which form centers (lit. circles) of energy at six major locations in the subtle body; it is through these centers that the ascending energy of *kundalinī* moves, purifying them and removing blockages

Chiti (*Citi*) the conscious, creative aspect of the supreme reality, often identified with the active, Goddess figure

Chitshakti (*Citśakti*) the creative power of I-consciousness or self-awareness

darshan (*darśana*) (lit. viewing) seeing or being in the presence of a revered person or sacred place; also, a system of philosophic affirmations and understandings

dhām (lit. abode)

dīkshā (*dīkṣā*) initiation, as in the imparting of a sacred mantra or the awakening of the aspirant's latent *kundalinī* energy through *shaktipāt*

ekāgratā concentration upon a single object; a pivotal technique in the yogic practice outlined by Patanjali, involving control of sense data and internal thought processes through a series of interrelated restraints and disciplines

Ganeshpuri a town fifty miles east of Bombay where Bhagavan Nityananda settled; the site of *Gurudev Siddha Peeth*, Swami Muktananda's main ashram

Gāvdevī one form of the Goddess, a representation of the creative, conscious aspect of supreme reality

gopī in the scriptural stories of young Krishna, the *gopī*s were the milkmaids of Vrindavan who formed intense devotional relationships with the Lord

Govinda a name for Krishna, especially the young cowherd of Vrindavan

guna (*guṇa*) one of the three modalities or qualities of all creation which permute and combine to create the observable mixtures of luminosity or intelligence (*sattva*), activity (*rajas*), and ignorance or inertia (*tamas*)

guru a master of spiritual initiation and guidance, whose cosmic func tion is identified in Kashmir Shaivism with the grace-bestowing power of God

Gurudev (lit. guru, Lord) a traditional term of address and reverence for one's guru

gurukripā (*gurukṛpā*) (lit. guru's grace) the transformative energy bestowed on a seeker by the guru, especially as in the process of initiation

hamsah (*haṁsaḥ*) (lit. I am That) a sacred mantra from the Vedas uniting and affirming the identity of the limited, bound self and the supreme reality; also, in Kashmir Shaivism, the natural, breath-linked mantra which is always being repeated by all persons

Īshwara (*Īśvara*) the Lord; the immanent aspect of supreme reality as it manifests with attributes and functions

jīvanmukti the state of the *jīvanmukta*, one who is liberated from the limitations of ego-consciousness while still remaining in the physical body; one traditional definition of the goal of *yoga*

jnāna (*jñāna*) the path of knowledge that is directed to the ultimate realities, to the highest understandings; hence, *jnānī* one who pursues the ultimate through the path of discriminating what is real from what is illusory and thereby forms the basis of a stable unity awareness

Jnaneshwar (*Jnāneśvara*) a thirteenth century Maharashtran poet-saint

karma (lit. action, work) actions and the consequences of one's prior actions; hence, destiny

khecharī mudrā (*khecarī mudrā*) a yogic and tantric practice, involving blockage of the air passages by turning the tongue back into the cavum

koān a consciousness-expanding question (e.g., "What is the sound of one hand clapping?") or object of contemplation (e.g., Mu), used as a teaching technique in Zen schools of Buddhism

Krishna (*Kṛṣṇa*) a human representation of the divine, an avatar or incarnation of the Lord, whose life story is depicted in the *Srimad Bhagavatam* and the *Mahabharata*

kriyā physical or mental purificatory movement of the awakened *kundalinī*

kumbhaka (*kuṁbhaka*) voluntary or involuntary retention of breath

kumkum red-colored powder made from turmeric, used for putting a mark of worship between the eyebrows

kundalinī (*kuṇḍalinī*) (lit. coiled one) the primal energy of the universe, some part of which is understood to be lying, coiled in a potential form, at the base of the spine and to be capable of being awakened and serving as the basis of spiritual evolution leading toward final union or realization

lungi an article of clothing commonly worn by men in India, a piece of cloth tied around the waist

Mahābhārata an epic compiled in the sixth and fifth centuries B.C., to which were added numerous other texts including the *Bhagavad Gita*

Mahāmāyā (lit. the great illusion) a name for Shakti, the creative conscious energy of the universe

Mahārāj (lit. great ruler) a term of respect used generally for highly esteemed persons

Maharashtra a state in the middle section of the Western coast of India, in which are located Bombay and Ganeshpuri

mahāvākya (lit. the great statement) one of the four central proclamations of the Upanishadic tradition, as synthesized by Shankarāchārya: Brahman is consciousness; the Atman is Brahman; I am Brahman; and Thou art That; together these affirm that the Supreme Reality (Brahman) is the Self of all, the supreme "I" and ground of existence

mandir (lit. temple)

Mangalore a state on the West coast of India, south of Maharashtra, the birthplace of Swami Muktananda

mantra (lit. that which protects) mystical sounds or phonemes, discovered in states of deep meditation, which are understood to express and be one with the underlying or primal levels of reality; therefore, in repeating such a mantra, one can contact the consciousness of those teachers whose lineage has adopted the mantra as a form of initiation and transformation

mārga (lit. path)

māyā (from the root *mā*, to measure) that which does not exist; therefore, illusory; also, the finitizing or limiting principle

moksha (*mokṣa*) liberation from the sense of duality and limitation

mudrā in *yoga*, a psychophysical process of sealing up energy and attention; also, a pose conveying emotions or blessings

mūlādhāra in yogic anatomy, the first psychic center or *chakra*, located at the base of the spine, which is the seat of the *kundalinī* power

nāda (lit. sound)

nādī (*nāḍī*) in yogic anatomy, any pathway or channel

Namah Shivāya (*Namah Śivāya*) (lit. salutations to Shiva) the five-syllable Vedic mantra, meaning "I honor my Inner Self"

Nārada a sage who expounded the path of divine love or *bhakti*

neela (*nīla*) (lit. blue)

neela bindu (*nīlabindu*) (lit. the blue point) the Blue Pearl

Neelakantha (*Nīlakanṭha*) (lit. the blue-throated one) a designation of Shiva

nirvikalpa the thought-free state

Nityananda (lit. the bliss of eternity) Swami Muktananda's guru

Nivrittināth (*Nivṛttinātha*) the older brother and guru of the poet-saint Jnaneshwar

OM a representation of the fundamental creative impulse of the Supreme; the basis of all mantras

Parabrahman the Absolute; Paramashiva

paramahamsa (*paramahaṁsa*) *hamsa* is the individual soul which reflects the cosmic polarity of *ham* (the self) and *sa* (the other); a *paramahamsa* is thus one who has resolved this polarity through self-realization

Paramashiva (*Paramaśiva*) the Absolute; also, *Parāshiva Paramātmā* the Lord

Paramātmāshakti (*Paramātmāśakti*) the conscious, creative power of the Absolute; also, *Parāshakti*

Pārvatī the supreme, conscious creative power, depicted as a Goddess; in mythology, the wife of Shiva

Patanjali (*Patañjali*) the author of the Yoga Sutras

prājna (*prājña*) the third body or the third state of consciousness, the causal state; also, in Vedānta, the intellectual sheath

prāna (*prāṇa*) a generic name for the vital force of all living beings and the entire cosmos; sometimes refers specifically to the breath

prānashakti (*prāṇaśakti*) the power of prana

prānāyāma (*prāṇāyāma*) (lit. regulation of prana) the practices or phenomena of the regulation of the vital force

Pratyabhijnāhridayam (*Pratyabhijñāhṛdayam*) (lit. the heart of recognition) the summarized text, by Kṣemarāja, of the *Pratyabhijna* philosophy which holds that to experience one's essential divinity one has only to recognize it

Purāna the collected corpus of Indian mythology

purusha (*puruṣa*) the individual experiencer or person; the subjective pole of differentiated consciousness

Rāma a name of God; an incarnation who is the hero of the epic *Ramayana*

Ramakrishna a nineteenth century Bengali saint who worshipped the divine in the form of the Mother

rudrāksha (*rudrākṣa*) rosary beads made from *Elaeocarpus Ganitrus*, a fruit with medicinal powers

Sadguru (lit. the true guru); and *Sadgurunath* (lit. the Lord sadguru)

sādhanā (lit. effort or means) refers to the efforts made by a seeker; also the means or path used for spiritual attainment; thus, *sādhaka,* one who has consciously embarked upon a spiritual path

sādhu a term of respect, especially for holy men

saguna (*saguṇa*) having a form

sahaj (*sahaja*) (lit. easy, spontaneous)

sahajāvasthā the sahaj state; the experience of the natural state of the Self which results when all obstacles to such experience are removed

sahasrāra (lit. one thousand petalled) the goal of the ascent of the *kundalinī* power, an ecstatic union of the Shiva-Shakti polarity depicted in yogic anatomy as a blazing thousand-petalled lotus in the cranial region

Saī (*svāmī*) (lit. master) a term of honor and respect

samādhi in *yoga,* a state of absorption of the mind; also, the tomb of a yogi or saint

sannyāsin one who has renounced the world and taken the vows of a monk

Sanskrit (*saṁskṛta*) (lit. complete) the language of the ancient Indian texts

saptāh (lit. seven days or a week) observances or celebrations, e.g., long chants

Sarasvatī the aspect of the divine relating to the arts, philosophy, and oratory, depicted as the Goddess

Sarvajnaloka Sarvajñaloka (lit. the region of omniscience) the state of omniscience

Satchidānanda (*saccidānanda*) (lit. absolute existence, consciousness, and bliss) the three indivisible categories used to describe the experience of the absolute

Shaivism the system of practices and understandings that center on Shiva as the representative of the supreme absolute; hence, a Shaivite, a follower of the path of Shaivism

Shakti (*Śakti*) (lit. power) the conscious creative power which becomes everything in the universe; the dynamic pole of the Shiva-Shakti polarity in all existence

shaktipāt (*śaktipāta*) (lit. the descent of power) the bestowal of grace; in Shaivism, a necessary precondition to spiritual advancement through the awakening of the *kundalinī* energy *shāmbhavī* (*śāṁbhavī*) a state of inner absorption with eyes half closed

Shankarāchārya an Indian philosopher-mystic who expounded the nondualistic teachings of Advaita Vedānta

Shirdi a village in Maharashtra made famous by the great Siddha, Sai Baba, who settled there in the late nineteenth century

Shiva (*Śiva*) the basis of the entire cosmos; the underlying reality, sometimes depicted as the primal Lord

shivo'ham (*śivo'ham*) (lit. I am Shiva) a description of the unitive experience; also, a mantra which affirms that unity

Shree (*Śrī*) a term of respect

Siddha (lit. complete, perfect) an adept, one who has completed the spiritual journey

Siddhaloka (lit. the world of Siddhas)

siddhi (lit. attainment or mastery) sometimes used to refer to occult powers

so'ham (lit. He am I) a description of the state of unification with the divine; also, a mantra affirming that identity

Sufi a mystic in the Islamic tradition

Suki a village close to Ganeshpuri where Muktananda was sent by his guru to meditate and where the Blue Pearl experiences took place

supracausal the fourth or *turīya* state, in which the unity of all form is experienced, as in the vision of the Blue Pearl

sushumnā (*suṣumnā*) in yogic anatomy one of the central channels in the subtle body through which the *kundalinī* power ascends when awakened

sushupti (*suṣupti*) the third state of consciousness, characterized by dreamless sleep

sūtra an aphoristic statement in a philosophic text

swāmi (*svāmi*) (lit. master) a monastic title

tandrā as used in Muktananda's *Play of Consciousness*, a visionary, meditative state; therefore, *tandrāloka*, the state of tandra

tantra scriptures attributed to a revelation by Lord Shiva, emphasizing the techniques and direct experiences associated with a nondualistic understanding of reality

tapas (lit. heat) the intensity generated by spiritual practice or austerities; therefore, *tapasya*, the practice of austerities

Trika (lit. threefold) the North Indian school of monistic Shaivism which analyzes the spiritual truths in terms of triads, one of which describes the spiritual process via the triad of the seeker, the sense of bondage, and the ultimate goal of unity consciousness

Tukāram a seventeenth century Maharashtran poet-saint who worshipped the Lord in the form of Vitthal

turīya (lit. the fourth) the fourth state of consciousness which is characterized by a sense of witnessing the experiences of the other three states

turīyātīta (lit. beyond the fourth) the final spiritual experience, characterized by an absence of any fundamental sense of difference; unity awareness

Umā (lit. the splendor of Shiva) the supreme power of the Lord, depicted as his consort

Upanishad (*Upaniṣad*) (lit. to sit down near) secret mystical knowledge imparted through the oral tradition; the latter part of each *Veda*

Vasugupta a Shaivite sage of Northern India who lived in the eighth or ninth century A.D.; he is credited with recording the revelation called the Shiva Sutras

Veda ancient sacred scriptures of India

Vedānta (lit. the end of the *Veda*) the mystical teachings drawn from the Upanishads; one of the six major Indian philosophies

veena (*vīnā*) a lute with a long stem and a gourd on each end

Vishnu (*Viṣnu*) the sustaining aspect of supreme reality, personified as one of the three divine figures, together with Brahma and Shiva

yoga realization of the unity of the individual and the divine; also, practices leading to this realization; hence, *yogī*, one who practices *yoga*

yoginī, a female *yogī*

BIBLIOGRAPHY

Aiyar, K. Narayanasvami. *Thirty Minor Upanishads.* Madras: Annie Besant, 1914.

Avalon, Arthur [Sir John Woodroffe]. *Principles of Tantra: The Tantra-Tattva of Śri Yukta Śiva Candra Vidyārṇava Bhattācārya Mahodaya. Part II.* 5th ed. Madras: Ganesh & Co., 1978.

———. *The Serpent Power: Being the Ṣaṭ-Cakra-Nirūpaṇa and Pādukā-Pañcaka.* Reprint. New York: Dover Publications, 1974.

———. *Shakti and Shākta.* 1918. Reprint. New York: Dover, 1978.

———, trans. and commentator. *Tantra of the Great Liberation: Mahānirvāna Tantra.* 1913. Reprint. New York: Dover Publications, 1972.

The Bhagavad Gita. Translated by Swami Nikhilananda. New York: Ramakrishna-Vivekananda Center, 1952.

Bhaktivedanta, A. C., trans. *Śrī Caitanya-Caritāmṛta of Kṛṣṇadāsa Kavirāja Gosvāmi.* 17 vols. New York: Bhaktivedanta Book Trust, 1974–75.

Bharati, Agehananda. *The Light at the Center: Context and Pretext of Modern Mysticism.* Santa Barbara, Cal.: Ross-Erikson, 1976.

———. *The Tantric Tradition.* Rev. Amer. ppb. ed. New York: Samuel Weiser, 1975.

Bohm, David. "The Enfolding-Unfolding Universe and Consciousness." In *Wholeness and the Implicate Order,* pp. 172–213. London: Routledge & Kegan Paul, 1980.

———. "Hidden Variables in the Quantum Theory." In *Wholeness and the Implicate Order*, pp. 65–110. London: Routledge & Kegan Paul, 1980.

———. *Quantum Theory*. New York: Prentice-Hall, 1951.

———. "Quantum Theory as an Indication of a New Order in Physics; Part B: Implicate and Explicate Order in Physical Law." In *Wholeness and the Implicate Order*, pp. 140–171. London: Routledge & Kegan Paul, 1980.

Bohm, David, and Weber, Renée. "Of Matter and Meaning: The Super-Implicate Order." *Re-Vision* 6(1983):34–44.

Chatterji, Jagadish Chandra. *Kashmir Shaivism*. 1914. Reprint. Srinagar: Research and Publication Department, Government of Jammu and Kashmir, 1962.

Chethimattam, John B. *Consciousness and Reality: An Indian Approach to Metaphysics*. Maryknoll, N.Y.: Orbis, 1971.

Coomaraswamy, Ananda K. "The Dance of Shiva." In *The Dance of Shiva: Fourteen Indian Essays*. Rev. ed. New Delhi: Sagar Publications, 1968.

Einstein, A.; Podolsky, B.; and Rosen, N. "Can Quantum-Mechanical Description of Physical Reality Be Considered Complete?" *Physical Review*, 47 (1935):777–780.

Eliade, Mircea. *Yoga: Immortality and Freedom*. 2nd ed. Princeton: Princeton University Press, 1969.

Eliade, Mircea. *Yoga: Immortality and Freedom*. Translated by Willard R. Trask. Princeton: Princeton University Press, Bollingen Paperback, 1970.

Fox, Matthew. *Breakthrough: Meister Eckhart's Creation Spirituality in a New Translation*. Garden City, N. Y.: Doubleday, 1980.

Freedman, Stuart, and Clauser, John. "Experimental Test of Local Hidden Variable Theories." *Physical Review Letters* 28 (1972): 938–941.

Gheranda Samhita. Translated by Rai Bahadur Srisa Chandra Vasu. 2nd ed. New Delhi: Oriental Books Reprint, 1975.

Guru Gita. In *Shree Guru Gita*. South Fallsburg, N.Y.: SYDA Foundation, 1981.

Hariharananda Aranya, Swami. *Yoga Philosophy of Patañjali*. Translated by P. N. Mukerji. Albany: State University of New York Press, 1983.

Hill, W. Douglas P. *The Holy Lake of the Acts of Rāma: An English Translation of Tulasī Dās's Rāmacaritamānasa*. London: Oxford University Press, 1952.

Īshvara-Pratyabhijñā-Vimarshinī of Utpaladeva. Edited by Pandit Mukund Rām Shāstrī. Kashmir Series of Texts and Studies #22. Srinagar: Research Department, Jammu & Kashmir State, 1918.

M. *The Gospel of Ramakrishna*. Translated by Swami Nikhilananda. New York: Ramakrishna Center, 1942.

Mouni Sadhu. *In Days of Great Peace: The Highest Yoga as Lived.* Hollywood, Cal.: Wilshire Book Company, 1974.

Muktananda, Swami. *Ashram Dharma.* Ganeshpuri, District Thana, Maharashtra, India: Shree Gurudev Ashram, 1975.

———. *Bhagawan Nityananda: His Life and Mission.* Ganeshpuri, District Thana, Maharashtra, India: Shree Gurudev Ashram, 1972.

———. "Guru, Kundalini, and the Inner Experience." Xeroxed transcript. Intensive talk, SYDA Foundation, South Fallsburg, N.Y., October 28, 1979.

———. *I am That: The Science of Hamsa from Vijnana Bhairava(24).* South Fallsburg, N.Y.: SYDA Foundation, 1978.

———. *In the Company of a Siddha: Interviews and Conversations with Swami Muktananda.* Oakland, Cal.: S.Y.D.A. Foundation, 1978.

———. *Kundalini: The Secret of Life.* South Fallsburg, N.Y.: SYDA Foundation, 1979.

———. *Lalleshwari: Spiritual Poems by a Great Siddha Yogini.* South Fallsburg, N.Y.: SYDA Foundation, 1981.

———. *Light on the Path.* Ganeshpuri, District Thana, Maharashtra, India: Shree Gurudev Ashram, 1972.

———. *Mystery of the Mind.* South Fallsburg, N.Y.: SYDA Foundation, 1982.

———. *The Perfect Relationship.* South Fallsburg, N.Y.: SYDA Foundation, 1980.

———. *Play of Consciousness (Chitshakti Vilas).* 2nd ed. San Francisco: Harper and Row, 1978.

———. *Reflections of the Self.* South Fallsburg, N.Y.: SYDA Foundation, 1980.

———. *Secret of the Siddhas.* South Fallsburg, N.Y.: SYDA Foundation, 1980.

———. *Siddha Meditation: Commentary on the Shiva Sutras and other Sacred Texts.* Oakland, Cal.: S.Y.D.A. Foundation, 1975.

———. *Where are You Going? A Guide to the Spiritual Journey.* South Fallsburg, N.Y.: SYDA Foundation, 1981.

Narada Sutras: The Philosophy of Love. Translated with a commentary by Hari Prasad Shastri. 2nd ed. London: Shanti Sadan, 1963.

Osborne, Arthur. *Ramana Maharshi and the Path of Self-Knowledge.* New York: Samuel Weiser, 1970.

Pagels, Elaine. *The Gnostic Gospels.* New York: Random House, 1979.

Pandey, Kanti Chandra. *Abhinavagupta: An Historical and Philosophical Study.* The Chowkhamba Sanskrit Studies, vol. 1. 2nd ed. Benares: The Chowkhamba Sanskrit Series Office, 1963.

Pandit, M. P. *Kulārṇava Tantra*. 2nd ed. Madras: Ganesh & Co., 1973.

Pearce, Joseph Chilton. *The Bond of Power*. New York: E. P. Dutton, 1981.

Pratyabhijñāhṛdayam: The Secret of Self-Recognition. Translated and annotated by Jaidev Singh. 3rd ed. rev. Delhi: Motilal Banarsidass, 1980.

Pribram, Karl. "What the Fuss is All About." In *The Holographic Paradigm and Other Paradoxes: Exploring the Leading Edge of Science*, edited by Ken Wilber, pp. 27–34. Boulder, Col.: Shambhala Publications, 1982.

Puthoff, Harold, and Targ, Russell. "Psychic Research and Modern Physics." In *Psychic Exploration: A Challenge for Science*, edited by John White, pp. 524–542. New York: Capricorn Books, G. P. Putnam, 1976.

Radhakrishnan, S, ed. and trans. *The Principal Upaniṣads*. London: George Allen & Unwin, 1953.

Radhakrishnan, Sarvepalli, and Moore, Charles A. *A Source Book in Indian Philosophy*. Princeton, N.J.: Princeton University Press, 1957.

Ramayana of Valmiki. Translated by Hari Prasad Shastri. 3 vols. London: Shanti Sadan, 1957.

Rudrappa. J. *Kashmir Shaivism*. Prasaranga: University of Mysore, 1969.

Schurmann, Reiner. *Meister Eckhart: Mystic and Philosopher*. Bloomington, Indiana: Indiana University, 1978.

Shankaracharya. *Aparokshānubhūti or Self-Realization of Sri Sankaracharya*. 1938. Translated by Swami Vimuktananda. 4th impression. Mayavati: Advaita Ashrama, 1973.

———. *Ātmabodha*. Translated by Swami Nikhilananda. *Self-Knowledge* (Ātmabodha). New York: Ramakrishna-Vivekananda Center, 1970.

———. *Vivekacūḍāmaṇi of Śrī Śaṅkarācārya*. Translated by Swami Madhavananda. 9th ed. Mayavati: Advaita Ashrama, 1974.

Sharma, L. N. *Kashmir Śaivism*. Benares: Bharatiya Vidya Prakashan, 1972.

Shree Gurudev Ashram. "Baba with Physicists: Dr. Harold Puthoff and Dr. Russell Targ." *Shree Gurudev Ashram Newsletter* Ganeshpuri, Dist. Thana, India 4, no. 7 (1975):6–12.

Shree Gurudev Ashram. "A Conversation with Baba," *Shree Gurudev Ashram Newsletter* Ganeshpuri, Dist. Thana, India 4, no. 6 (1975):5–9.

Singh, Jaidev, trans. and ed. *Pratyabhijñāhṛdayam: The Secret of Self-Recognition*. 3rd ed. rev. Delhi: Motilal Banarsidass, 1980.

———, trans. and ed. *Śiva Sūtras: The Yoga of Supreme Identity*. Delhi: Motilal Banarsidass, 1979.

———, trans. and ed. *Spanda-Kārikās: The Divine Creative Pulsation*. Delhi: Motilal Banarsidass, 1980.

Sinh, Pancham, trans. *The Hatha Yoga Pradipika*. 1915. Reprint. New York: AMS Press, 1974.

Śiva Mānasa Pūjā. In *The Nectar of Chanting*, pp. 140–143. Oakland, Cal.: S.Y.D.A. Foundation, 1975.

Siva Samhita. Translated by Rai Bahadur Srisa Chandra Vasu. 2nd ed. New Delhi: Oriental Books Reprint, 1975.

Śiva Sūtras: The Yoga of Supreme Identity. Translated and edited by Jaidev Singh. Delhi: Motilal Banarsidass, 1979.

Śiva-Mahimnaḥ Stotram. In *The Nectar of Chanting*, pp. 118–139. Oakland, Cal.: S.Y.D.A. Foundation, 1975.

Spanda-Kārikās: The Divine Creative Pulsation. Translated and edited by Jaidev Singh. Delhi: Motilal Banarsidass, 1980.

Srimad Bhagavatam. Translated by Kamala Subramaniam. Bombay: Bharatiya Vidya Bhavan, 1979.

Tantrāloka of Abhinava Gupta with Commentary by Rājānaka Jayaratha. Vol. 1. Edited by Pandit Mukund Rām Shāstrī. Kashmir Series of Texts and Studies #23. Srinagar: Research Department, Jammu & Kashmir State, 1918.

Targ, Russell, and Puthoff, Harold. *Mind-Reach: Scientists Look at Psychic Ability*. New York: Delacourte Press, 1977.

Vishnu Tirtha Maharaj, Swami. *Devatma Shakti: (Kundalini) Divine Power*. 2nd ed. Bombay: Shri Sadhan Granthmala Prakashan, 1962.

Weber, Renée. "The Enfolding-Unfolding Universe: A Conversation with David Bohm." In *The Holographic Paradigm and Other Paradoxes: Exploring the Leading Edge of Science*, edited by Ken Wilber, pp. 44–104. Boulder, Col.: Shambhala Publications, 1982.

Wilber, Ken. *The Atman Project: A Transpersonal View of Human Development*. Wheaton, Ill.: Theosophical Publishing House, 1980.

———. *No Boundary: Eastern and Western Approaches to Personal Growth*. Boulder, Col.: Shambhala Publications, 1981.

———. "Odyssey: A Personal Inquiry into Humanistic and Transpersonal Psychology." *Journal of Humanistic Psychology* 22 (1982):57–90.

———. "Physics, Mysticism, and the New Holographic Paradigm: A Critical Appraisal." In *The Holographic Paradigm and Other Paradoxes: Exploring the Leading Edge of Science*, edited by Ken Wilber, pp. 157–186. Boulder, Col.: Shambhala Publications, 1982.

———. *The Spectrum of Consciousness*. Wheaton, Ill.: Theosophical Publishing House, 1977.

———. *Up from Eden: A Transpersonal View of Human Evolution*. Garden City, N.Y.: Anchor Press/Doubleday, 1981.

———, ed. *The Holographic Paradigm and Other Paradoxes: Exploring the Leading Edge of Science*. Boulder, Col.: Shambhala Publications, 1982.

———, ed. *Eye to Eye: The Quest for the New Paradigm*. Garden City, N.Y.: Anchor Press/Doubleday, 1983.

Woodroffe, Sir John. [Arthur Avalon, pseud.] *The Garland of Letters: Studies in the Mantra-Śāstra*. 7th. ed. Pondicherry, India: Ganesh & Co., 1979.

NOTES

In preparing the text of the manuscript and notes, I have developed a system of diacritical marks that strikes a balance between several considerations. On the one hand, I have written the Romanized version of some Sanskrit words to indicate how they are pronounced. For example, *Śakti* is written as *Shakti* and *cit* as *chit* because, otherwise, anyone unfamiliar with the Sanskrit diacritical marks would be either confused or misled by the traditional way of writing such words. On the other hand, I have included all macrons, the bars over some vowels, because omitting them would sometimes lead to ambiguity and error. For example, *sādhana* and *sādhanā*, which have rather different meanings, would be indistinguishable if the macrons were not shown. Furthermore, it is helpful for pronunciation to know that the macron indicates a long vowel. All diacritical marks other than the macron have been omitted, except that I have preserved whatever diacritical system is used in the titles of works cited and in the excerpts drawn from *Play of Consciousness* and other sources. One misleading way of transposing Marathi into Roman script that recurs throughout *Play of Consciousness* has been altered to a more customary procedure; it involves using an "ḷ" instead of an "ṛ", thus bringing several key words in line with the Sanskrit terms that they parallel (for example, *nīṛa* becomes *nīḷa*). In the Glossary, I present in parentheses the Sanskrit version of each entry with all diacritical marks included when that differs from how the entry appears throughout the manuscript.

PREFACE

1 Swami Muktananda, *Play of Consciousness (Chitshakti Vilas)*, 2nd ed. (San Francisco: Harper & Row, 1978). All page references to *Play of Consciousness* refer to this edition.

2 The most comprehensive introduction to transpersonal psychology can be found in the work of Ken Wilber. His first book, *Spectrum of Consciousness*, develops a hierarchical model for human awareness and integrates contemporary psychological commentary with traditional Eastern formulations of higher states of consciousness. His next book, *No Boundary*, is an effort to present this model in a more popular form and apply it to the procedures and goals of therapeutic techniques. *The Atman Project* traces individual development from birth to enlightenment, showing the oscillation between approach and resistance to the ultimate. In *Up from Eden* Wilber examines cultural and societal evolution from prehistory to the present and concludes that they demonstrate a gradually rising level of awareness for both the geniuses of a culture and, several levels lower, the bulk of humanity. Two collections, edited by Wilber, contain some of his most important essays: *The Holographic Paradigm* and *Eye to Eye*. A compelling and personal narrative of Wilber's development is found in his article, "Odyssey."

In addition to *Re-Vision*, a journal edited by Wilber, the major sources for articles on transpersonal psychology are *The Journal of Transpersonal Psychology*, *Journal of Humanistic Psychology*, and *Parabola*. A professional society, The Association for Transpersonal Psychology, holds annual meetings, publishes a journal, and keeps track of the slowly growing opportunities for undergraduate and graduate work in this area. The address for the Association is P.O. Box 3049, Stanford, California 94305. Another professional society with highly congruent interests is the Association for Humanistic Psychology, located at 325 Ninth Street, San Francisco, California 94103.

CHAPTER TWO: *Images of Power and Purification*

1 Shree Gurudev Ashram, "Baba with Physicists," p. 11.

2 *Bindu* literally means "point" or "drop." In the Shaivite texts, it is understood to be the compacted sphere of all potential. (See Raghava Bhatta's fifteenth century commentary on the *Shāradā Tilak*, an eleventh century text by Lakshmanacharya, as cited in Woodroofe, *The Garland of Letters*, p. 132, and in Avalon, *Shakti and Shākta*, chap. 19. See also *Parātrimshikā*, as cited in Jaideva Singh, *Pratyabhijñāhṛdayam*, p. 7.) The absolute, *Paramashiva*, through polarization into Shiva-Shakti or *prakāsha-vimarsha* starts the process of manifestation or *ābhāsa*. This manifestation is the objective pole and is called the Shakti or the power of the absolute. This objectivization occurs within supreme consciousness or *chit*, but, to the polarized consciousness, it seems

to occur outside. (See Singh, *Pratyabhijñāhṛdayam,* Sutra 2, and also Singh's citation of *Īshvara pratyabhijñā,* p. 19.) At the same time, the subjective pole, Shiva, is defined, through a process of self-limitation, into the limited human consciousness. (For his commentary on Sutra 9 of *Pratyabhijñāhṛdayam,* see Swami Muktananda, *Siddha Meditation* and see also *Tattvasandoha,* as cited in Woodroffe, *Garland,* chap. 15.)

The polarization starts as an impulse (*spanda*) to become this and all other worlds. This impulse, in turn, generates the necessary creative stress (*nāda*). This creative stress gathers as a point which contains in it the germ of all possibilities. (See *Tattvasandoha,* as cited in Woodroffe, *Garland,* p. 109.) This point is the *bindu.* It is not a point in time and space. It is the point at which the objective pole of creative consciousness, or *Chitshakti,* has become clear, and it is likened to an artist's conception of what he is about to paint. This conception is perceived as a "something" within supreme consciousness and hence this level is also characterized by a sense of "this," or *idam.* Like an artist who knows what his creation is going to be, Shiva knows perfectly what he is going to manifest. Hence, this stage of creation is dominated by *jnāna shakti* or the power of perfect knowing. (See Rajanaka Ananda, in his *Vivaraṇa,* as cited in Singh, *Pratyabhijñāhṛdayam,* p. 11.) Finally, because creation is taking shape within it, the *bindu* is also called *ghanibhūta Shakti* or the *Shakti* becoming "dense." (See *Prapañcasāra Tantra,* as cited in Woodroffe, *Garland,* p. 132.)

Beyond this stage, as the experience crystallizes within supreme consciousness, the sense of otherness becomes more and more defined (*sphuta*) until, as in the limited human experience, the subject feels distinct from and unrelated to the contents of consciousness. (See Woodroffe, *Garland,* chap. 10, and see also *Īshvara Pratyabhijñā,* as cited in Woodroffe, *Garland,* p. 172). Creation is not a one-time process. It is continuous, but this in no way detracts from the essential unity of all consciousness. Shiva, the cosmic artist, is constantly creating from his own being, without losing his identity. (See Muktananda's commentary on the *Īshvara Pratyabhijñā* 11/12 in his *Siddha Meditation,* p. 71.) Shiva conceives the universe within himself through his own power or Shakti. This very act of conception is sufficient to create everything; it is the creative act (*srishti-kalpanā*) whose result (*parināma*) is what we consider the world. (See Woodroffe, *Garland,* pp. 22–23.) This conception is an ecstatic outburst of creativity (See Kshemaraja, as cited in Singh, *Pratyabhijñāhṛdayam,* p. 10) or a surveying of his own splendor. (See Maheshvarananda's *Mahārthmañjarī,* as cited in Singh, *Pratyabhijñāhṛdayam,* p. 9.)

The *bindu,* though a unitary experience within supreme consciousness, appears at the individual level for each meditator until there arises the realization that there is only the one supreme consciousness. Hence the Shaivite saying: "As here, so there." (*Śiva Sūtras* 3.14) (For two complementary perspectives on this aphorism, see Kshemarāja's commentary on Sutra 4, as cited in Singh *Pratyabhijñāhṛdayam,* p. 56, and *Vishvasāra Tantra,* as cited in Woodroffe, *Garland,* p. 94.) We re-enact the cosmic processes individually. (See Muktananda's commentary on Sutra 10 of *Pratyabhijñāhṛdayam* in his *Siddha Meditation*). However, as when seeing one object reflected in a hall of mirrors, we fail to comprehend that we are looking at the multiple reflections of the one supreme actor.

3 Muktananda, *Play of Consciousness,* p. 28.
4 Mircea Eliade, *Yoga,* p. 4.
5 Reiner Schurmann, *Meister Eckhart,* pp. 114–121, 159–163.
6 John B Chethimattam, *Consciousness and Reality,* pp. 172–181.
7 *Yoga* comes from the Sanskrit root *yuj* which means "to yoke" or "to join." It refers to the joining of the individual soul (*jīvātman*) and the universal soul (*paramātman*). (See Avalon, *Tantra of the Great Liberation* 14.123.) As used in most contexts, *yoga* could refer to (a) the practices which effect this union of *jīvātman* and *paramātman;* (b) the phenomena, experiences, and powers (*siddhis*) occurring as a result of yogic practices, or (c) the goal of *yoga,* which is liberation, (*jīvanmukti* or *moksha*).

Yoga is also considered to be a *darshana,* one of the six classical views of reality in Indian philosophy. (See Sarvepalli Radhakrishnan and Charles A. Moore, *A Source Book in Indian Philosophy,* chap. 13.) Sometimes *bhakti* (devotion), *karma* (selfless service), and *jnāna* (knowledge) are also referred to as forms of *yoga;* however, even though these three are complete spiritual paths in themselves, they are not technically *yoga* in the restricted sense used here. (See Mircea Eliade, *Yoga,* for further discussion on the yogic tradition.)

The three major forms of *yoga* referred to in this volume are: Patanjali's *yoga,* a version emphasizing yogic anatomy and subtle energies, and Muktananda's synthesis, which he calls Siddha Yoga. The first of these, the classical system described in Patanjali's *Yoga Sutras,* is based on Sāmkhya philosophy. (See Hariharananda, *Yoga Philosophy of Patañjali.*) Also called *ashtānga* (eight-limbed) *yoga,* it has eight major steps in its practice: moral observances (do's and don'ts), cleansing and strengthening practices, and absorption (*samādhi*), culminating in freedom or *kaivalya.*

The second version of *yoga* is described in the Upanishads (particularly *Yogatattva, Dhyānabindu,* and *Nādabindu*). (See Aiyar, *Thirty Minor Upanishads.*) It is also found in such other texts as *Śiva Samhitā, Haṭhayoga Pradīpikā, Gheranda Samhitā,* and *Ṣat-Cakra-Nirūpana* (Avalon, *Serpent Power*). One distinguishing characteristic of this approach is its emphasis on subtle yogic anatomy (*chakra* and *nādī*) and the *kundalinī* power in the subtle body. *Yoga* practice, in this tradition, seeks to unite the polarized energies in the body-mind complex. A preliminary goal is to awaken the *kundalinī* energy, and this, in turn, leads to the union or *yoga* of the Shiva-Shakti polarity. The guru and, in some texts, the *mantra* play an essential role in these developments. (See Avalon. *Principles of Tantra*, Part 2, pp. 66–78.)

The third approach to *yoga*, described by Muktananda as Siddha Yoga, subsumes many of the features of the first two approaches. However, the distinguishing feature of this *yoga* is the overriding importance of the Siddha guru and the guru-disciple relationship. (See *Guru Gita* 76; also see Muktananda, *The Perfect Relationship*, pp. 1–7 and his *Play of Consciousness*, pp. 101–115.) Spiritual initiation (*dīkshā*) starts with the descent of *shakti* (*shaktipāt*) which is a form of the guru's grace (*gurukripā*). *Shaktipāt* awakens the *kundalinī* energy. (See Swami Vishnu Tirth, *Devatma Sakti*, chap. 9.) The resulting process (*sādhanā*) is both purificatory and expanding. Each ensuing experience (*kriyā*) occurs under the influence of the awakened *kundalinī* and is not brought about by any specific practices. (See Muktananda, *Play of Consciousness*, pp. 101–115.) The *kundalinī* is experienced as the inner guide, indistinguishably one's own Self and the divine. Nurturing this relationship culminates in final realization and perfection (Siddhahood). (See Muktananda, *Play of Consciousness*, pp. 182–194, and see also his commentary on *Śiva Sūtra* 3.13 in *Siddha Meditation*, pp. 61–62.) This state is a total encompassing (*vyāpti*) of supreme consciousness (*Paramashiva*) and engages both the immanent and transcendent aspects of the absolute. (See Muktananda's commentary on *Spanda Kārikā* in *Siddha Meditation*, pp. 85–86.)

8 Yogic anatomy refers to the traditional yogic description of the physical and subtle bodies and their role in the process of purification. The primary locus of the yogic work is in the subtle body (*sūkshma sharīra*), which is understood to be a coherent organization of thoughts, emotions, and conscious energy (*prāna*) flowing through a complex of channels (*nādīs*). These channels interconnect at junctions that, to the inner yogic vision, resemble wheels (*chakras*) or lotuses (*padmas*) of light. The subtle body and the physical body are understood to be interpenetrating, so that changes in one produce corresponding changes in the other. The source of the energy is a condensed center of partially active, but mainly dormant, power (*shakti*) called *kundalinī* (the coiled one). The psycho-physical functions of the human being are maintained by this partially active power. The *kundalinī* is the cosmic, intelligent energy, but in a human being *kundalinī* has three aspects of increasing subtlety, located at the base of the spine, the heart, and the top of the head. (See Muktananda, *Secret of the Siddhas*, p. 9.)

When, through grace and yogic practice, the *kundalinī* is uncoiled or awakened, the consciousness (*chitta*), vital force (*prāna*), and generative force (*bindu*) are channeled upward along the central *nādī* called the *sushumnā*. (See Sinh, *The Hatha Yoga Pradipika* 3.1 and 4.10; see also *Siva Samhita* 4.12–14.) As this proceeds, the energies are transmuted, and the six major *chakras* along the path of the *sushumnā* are "pierced" by the ascending *kundalinī* (*chakra bheda*). A gradual purification (*shuddhi*) of all levels of the seeker's consciousness is accompanied by a loosening of egocentric human consciousness until it expands into supreme consciousness (*Paramashiva*) when the *kundalinī* finally stabilizes at the *sahasrāra* (thousand petalled center) at the top of the head. (See Muktananda, *Kundalini.*) An excellent reference for yogic anatomy is the *Ṣat-Cakra-Nirūpana,* available in English as Avalon, *The Serpent Power.*

9 Swami Muktananda, "Guru, Kundalini, and the Inner Experience," p. 9.
10 Muktananda, "Guru, Kundalini, and the Inner Experience," p. 14.
11 Harold Puthoff and Russell Targ, "Psychic Research and Modern Physics," pp. 524–542; Russell Targ and Harold Puthoff, *Mind-Reach.*
12 Joseph Chilton Pearce, *The Bond of Power,* p. 34.
13 Ken Wilber, *The Atman Project,* pp. 40–42.
14 Muktananda, "Guru, Kundalini, and the Inner Experience," p. 13.
15 Elaine Pagels, *The Gnostic Gospels* pp. 119–140.
16 Matthew Fox, *Breakthrough,* pp. 23–42.
17 Two accounts by the same author, one formal and the other personal, provide an excellent introduction to the diverse Hindu and Buddhist forms of *tantra.* See Agehananda Bharati, *The Tantric Tradition* and *The Light at the Center.*

CHAPTER THREE: *Images of Devotion*

1 Shree Gurudev Ashram, "A Conversation with Baba," p. 7.
2 Shree Gurudev Ashram, "A Conversation with Baba," p. 7.
3 Swami Hariharananda Aranya, *Yoga Philosophy of Patañjali,* pp. 262–263; for an interesting discussion of the most relevant of Patanjali's *Yoga-sutras,* 3.11 and 3.12, see Mircea Eliade, *Yoga,* pp. 47–52.
4 *Bhakti* is devotion and surrender to a spiritual ideal; the spiritual ideal can be a teacher, a chosen deity, or anyone who is, to the devotee, a manifestation of the divine. The *bhakti* literature refers to different kinds of devotion; the higher kind (*mukhyā*) is its own reward and is both a means to and the goal of spirituality. (See *Narada Sutras* 26 and 30.) *Bhakti* covers the entire range of human emotions, from the pain of separation to the rapturous delights of direct encounter (*darshana*) to the ineffable experience of blissful union. In *bhakti,* every human emotion can be, and traditionally has been, directed toward the chosen deity. (See *Narada Sutras* 65, 82.) The practice of *bhakti* does not have any prerequisites; everyone is qualified. (See *Narada Sutras* 72–73 and *The Bhagavad Gita* 9.26–32.) In *bhakti* all paths lead to the truth, and the truth assumes whatever form is dear to the devotee. (See *The Bhagavad Gita* 4.11 and 7.21–22 and also *Śiva-Mahimnah Stotram* 7.) The practice of *bhakti* includes associating with saints and other devotees (*satsanga*), chanting and reciting sacred texts as a form of

self-study (*svādhyāya*), and ritual worship. (See *Narada Sutras* 36–37, 67–68.)

The easiest and most effective means for experiencing divine love is through the grace of the saints. (See *Narada Sutras* 38–39.) *Bhakti* texts point out that through devotion to the guru, who is, in essence, the supreme Self, the benefits of both *yoga* and *jnāna* are realized. (See *Guru Gita* 9, 21, 53, 69, 81, 98 and Muktananda, *Play of Consciousness* pp. 17–26.) As Patanjali recommends, it becomes possible to transcend human limitations by contemplating one who is beyond them. (See Sutra 1.37. in Hariharananda, *Yoga Philosophy*.)

The life of Chaitanya Mahaprabhu is a valuable record of the process and transformative power of *bhakti*. (See A. C. Bhaktivedanta, *Śrī Caitanya-Caritāmṛta*.) His state or feeling (*bhāva*) ranged from intense yearning for and adoration of Krishna to exalted, unitive states in which he displayed Krishna-like characteristics. Since *bhakti* draws on emotions that are experienced by the devotee, *bhakti* is usually taken to be more accessible and easier than the practices of *jnāna*. (See *The Bhagavad Gita* 12.5.) In the end, the devotee comes to realize that all, including himself, are expressions of the one truth. (See *The Bhagavad Gita* 6.29–30.) Thus, the goal of *bhakti* is identical to the goal of *jnāna*. At this level, *bhakti* is called *parābhakti* (transcendental devotion), as portrayed vividly by the *gopi*s' all consuming love for Krishna in the *Srimad Bhagavatam*. Similarly, Muktananda's invocation to his guru in *Play of Consciousness* and his essay on the nectar of Guru's love (*gurupremāmrita*) are both examples of *parābhakti*. (See Muktananda, *Play of Consciousness*, pp. xxxi–xxxii and *Light on the Path*, pp. 59–68.) The *Shiva Manasa Puja*, written by Shankarāchārya, who is generally remembered for his intellectual contributions in the formulation of Vedānta, is a noteworthy example of *bhakti* literature. The *Srimad Bhagavatam* and the *Ramayana* are sources of many traditional *bhakti* themes. (See especially the Tulsidas version in W. Douglas P. Hill, *The Holy Lake of the Acts of Rāma*.) Among more contemporary spiritual figures, the devotion of Ramakrishna Paramahamsa for the divine Mother is a particularly rich example of *bhakti*. (See M., *The Gospel of Ramakrishna*.)

5 Muktananda, *Play of Consciousness*, p. 64.
6 Muktananda, *Play of Consciousness*, p. 65.
7 Muktananda, *Play of Consciousness*, pp. 65–7.
8 Muktananda, *Play of Consciousness*, pp. 175–176.

CHAPTER FOUR: *Images of Understanding*

1 Muktananda, *Mystery of the Mind*, p. 9.
2 *Jnāna* means knowledge. A *jnānī* is one who knows. As used here, *jnāna* refers to the knowledge of the supreme reality, which is identical to the Self. (See *Chāndogya Upanishad* 6.8.7; all references to the

Upanishads in this note are to Sarvepalli Radhakrishnan, *The Principal Upanishads.*) Sometimes the supreme *jnāna* is referred to as *ātmavidyā* (self-knowledge), *parāvidyā* (transcendental knowledge), or *aparoksha jnāna* (direct knowledge) to differentiate it from empirical knowledge which can be binding. (See *Mundaka Upanishad* 1.1.4; *Kena Upanishad* 1.4–9 and 2.1–5; and *Śiva Sūtras* 1.2.)

Jnāna is a spiritual attainment in the sense that it is the culmination of the spiritual search. In another sense, *jnāna* is the process that leads to the supreme *jnāna,* and this process could take many forms, such as self-searching (*vicāra*) and contemplative thought (*tarka*). (See Shankarāchārya, *Aparokṣānubhūti* 11–12 and *Maitrī Upanishad* 6.20.)

The supreme *jnāna* is a recognition *(pratyabhijnā)* of one's true nature. (See *Īshvara-pratyabhijñā-vimarshinī* 1.1.1 and *Śiva Sūtras* 1.1). This knowledge is liberating and a state of complete identity with bliss-consciousness (*chidānanda*). (See *Śvetāśvatara Upanishad* 5.13 and *Pratyabhijñāhṛdayam* 16.) In fact, liberation (*moksha*) is defined as direct knowledge of one's divine nature. (See *Tantrāloka* 1.156.) This experience is also described as existence-consciousness-bliss absolute (*saccidānanda*). (See *Ātmabodha* 56.) It is an experience of perfect unity in the midst of apparent diversity. (See *Śvetāśvatara Upanishad* 3.1) It is perfect joy (*ānanda*) and fullness (*pūrnatva*). (See *Taittirīya Upanishad* 2.7 and also Sharma, *Kashmir Śaivism,* chap. 10.)

Through grace (*anugraha*), which is the divine power of self-revelation, *jnāna* arises spontaneously. (See Muktananda, *Secret of the Siddhas,* p. 193.) This is possible through the agency of a true guru (*sadguru*). (See Muktananda's commentary on *Shiva Sutra* 2.6, *"guru-rupaya,"* in *Siddha Meditation,* p. 54.)

Sometimes *bhakti, jnāna,* and *yoga* are considered separate, even mutually exclusive paths. From Muktananda's point of view, however, they not only lead to the same goal but, through the descent of grace on the seeker (*shaktipāt*), these three blend and mutually reinforce each other. (See Muktananda, *Kundalini* and *Play of Consciousness.*) Muktananda's writing on *jnāna* draws from two main traditions: Vedānta and Kashmir Shaivism. Standard texts in English for Vedānta are three works of Shankarāchārya, *Ātmabodha, Vivekacūḍāmaṇi,* and *Aparokṣānubhūti,* as well as the major Upanishads. Standard texts on Kashmir Shaivism are *Pratyabhijñāhṛdayam, Śiva Sūtras,* and *Spanda Kārikās.*

CHAPTER FIVE: *Transpersonal Psychology*

1 See A. Einstein, B. Podolsky, and N. Rosen, "Can Quantum-Mechanical Description of Physical Reality Be Considered Complete?" pp. 777–78; David Bohm, *Quantum Theory,* pp. 611–623; and Stuart Freedman and John Clauser, "Experimental Test of Local Hidden Variable Theories," pp. 938–941.

2 David Bohm, "Hidden Variables in the Quantum Theory," pp. 71–72.
3 David Bohm, "The Enfolding-Unfolding Universe and Consciousness," p. 175.
4 Wilber is correct in reminding us that, for Bohm, " . . . there is nothing mystical or transcendental about the implicate order." See Ken Wilber, "Physics, Mysticism, and the New Holographic Paradigm," pp. 168–179. However, the breadth of Bohm's interests and the power of the thinking he shares with the Indian teacher, Krishnamurti, make it inappropriate to limit his purview by insisting on a restricted portrait of his model's inspiration and potential applications.
5 Renée Weber, "The Enfolding-Unfolding Universe: A Conversation with David Bohm," pp. 62–68.
6 See David Bohm, "Quantum Theory as an Indication of a New Order in Physics," pp. 140–157; Karl Pribram, "What the Fuss is All About, " pp. 27–34.
7 David Bohm and Renée Weber, "Of Matter and Meaning," p. 40.
8 David Bohm and Renée Weber, "Of Matter and Meaning," p. 44.
9 To conclude, as I do here, that the absolute is best understood as the inherent tendency or principle of reality that manifests in and as the processes of purification, love, and understanding is to identify the absolute with what Kashmir Shaivism calls *anugraha* or grace. Shaivism, as Coomaraswamy spells out in "The Dance of Shiva," pp. 70–77, takes note of Shiva's five cosmic actions, the *pancakritya*: creation, preservation, destruction, concealment, and grace. Kashmir Shaivism, however, places particular emphasis on the latter two as evidence of the pure will of the Lord, expressing itself in a playful, bipolar sport of self-revelation and illusion or self-obscuration. See J. Rudrappa, *Kashmir Shaivism*, pp. 101–103 and 118–134 and Kanti Chandra Pandey, *Abhinavagupta*, pp. 442–443. Their discussion makes it clear that concealment (*tirodhāna*), no less than grace, is an inherent tendency and mode of manifestation of the absolute. I can appreciate such a position, but I prefer to dwell primarily on the function of grace that Muktananda identifies as the *gurutattva* or guru principle. Here, *tattva* refers to the inherent tendency or principle inferred from the processes of transformation; see Kanti Chandra Pandey, *Abhinavagupta*, pp. 357–358. It is thus the built-in "suchness" (or, literally, "that-ness") of all reality. The *gurutattva* is referred to in Kashmir Shaivism as the highest principle; see *Guru Gita*: 8, 74 and the *Kulārṇava Tantra* 3:113 (see M. P. Pandit, *Kulārṇava Tantra*, p. 46). Muktananda, in his discussion of the *gurutattva*, assimilates all five cosmic actions within the grace-bestowing power of God, as manifesting through the guru; see his *Siddha Meditation*, pp. 54 and 110. Thus, my discussion of the absolute reflects my inclination to see the guru principle as the clearest and most useful indication of the reality of the absolute in our daily life and its transformation.
10 Swami Muktananda, *In the Company of a Siddha*, pp. 141–146.

INDEX